GIANNI VATTIMO *and* RENÉ GIRARD

CHRISTIANITY, TRUTH, AND WEAKENING FAITH

A Dialogue

Edited by PIERPAOLO ANTONELLO

Translated by WILLIAM MCCUAIG

COLUMBIA UNIVERSITY PRESS NEW YORK

COLUMBIA UNIVERSITY PRESS

Publishers Since 1893

New York   Chichester, West Sussex

Originally published as *Verità o Fede Debole*, copyright © 2006 Pier Vittorio e Associati, Transeuropa, Massa

English translation copyright © 2010 Columbia University Press

English-language edition published by arrangement with Eulama Literary Agency, Rome

Library of Congress Cataloging-in-Publication Data

Vattimo, Gianni, 1936–

[Verita o fede debole. English]

Christianity, truth, and weakening faith : a dialogue / Gianni Vattimo and René Girard ; edited by Pierpaolo Antonello ; translated by William McCuaig.

p. cm.

Includes bibliographical references.

ISBN 978-0-231-14828-3 (cloth : alk. paper)—ISBN 978-0-231-52041-6 (e-book)

1. Christianity—Philosophy.   2. Christianity and culture.   3. Relativity.   I. Girard, René.   II. Antonello, Pierpaolo.   III. Title.

BR100.V3513   2010

261.2'1—dc22   2009025569

Columbia University Press books are printed on permanent and durable acid-free paper.

This book is printed on paper with recycled content.
Printed in the United States of America

c   10 9 8 7 6 5 4 3 2 1

CONTENTS

NOTE ON THE TEXT

The provenance of the chapters of this book is as follows:

EDITOR'S INTRODUCTION: Revised and expanded from the introduction to the Italian edition, *Verità o Fede Debole?*

CHAPTER 1, Gianni Vattimo and René Girard, "Christianity and Modernity." A debate between Girard and Vattimo held in the city of Pordenone on 25 September 2004, as part of the Pordenonelegge festival.

CHAPTER 2, Gianni Vattimo and René Girard, "Faith and Relativism." The final round-table debate of the conference "Identità e desiderio," on the work of René Girard in relation to the social sciences and literary theory. Falconara, Sala consigliare, 10 March 2006.

CHAPTER 3, Gianni Vattimo and René Girard, "Hermeneutics, Authority, Tradition." An "open discussion" on René Girard from a conference held at the Humanities Center of Stanford University on 12 and 13 April 1996. In the discussion, explicit reference is made to Vattimo's essay "Heidegger and Girard: *Kénosis* and the End of Metaphysics," which appears as chapter 4 in this book.

CHAPTER 4, Gianni Vattimo, "Heidegger and Girard: *Kénosis* and the End of Metaphysics." First published in German in B. Dieckmann, *Das Opfer—aktuelle Kontroversen. Religions-*

politischer Diskurs im Kontext der mimetischen Theorie. Münster: Lit Verlag, 1999. Vattimo originally drafted this text in English as a conference paper, and that text has been revised for this book by the translator.

CHAPTER 5, René Girard, "Not Just Interpretations, There Are Facts Too." Girard originally drafted this essay in English, and that text has been revised for this book by the translator.

CHRISTIANITY, TRUTH, AND WEAKENING FAITH

INTRODUCTION

Pierpaolo Antonello

Among the numerous "conflicts" that characterize contemporary philosophical and intellectual discourse, the one between laicism[1] and religion—between the need for democratic states to promote confessional pluralism and substantial relativism, and the supposedly peremptory, authoritarian, and hegemonic culture of the religions—is emerging as one of the most crucial and important. The debate on the laicity of the state in France or in Turkey, the theologization of politics in the United States, the discussion of so-called postsecular society in Germany, the ongoing debate in Italy about the relation between relativism and faith, and the polemical fury over the clash of science and religion sparked by Richard Dawkins's *The God Delusion* in Great Britain are all telling examples of a discussion that is growing ever more heated, and not just in the Western context. The problem is that, very often, these debates become polarized in a way that does more to encourage the spirit of disputation and journalistic simplification than it does to promote a precise and cogent articulation of the terms of the question: vociferous protagonists on both sides tend to emphasize, and not always in good faith, the "difference" between value systems and their proponents, whether laic and materialist on one hand (allegedly heirs of the Enlightenment or, rather, of an ingenuous scientism), or Christian and fideistic on the other. Their extremist tone has the paradoxical effect of reminding us that extremes tend to converge, and to sound alike.

There are other, less clamorous theoretical stances, though, that do not set up stockades or barriers on the field of battle but instead propose a theoretical and philosophical terrain that allows an effective reconciliation between religion and laicity, between the need to promote relativism within liberal society and acceptance of the importance of religions in people's private and public lives and in creating shared ethical foundations. This book is a contribution to this discussion from a perspective of this kind: it offers two voices in the contemporary intellectual debate that are engaged not in separating the two camps but in *uniting* them, on the basis of an intuition already partially elaborated by Max Weber, implicitly suggested and described by Eric Auerbach in *Mimesis*, and more recently argued by Marcel Gauchet, to the effect that secularization—and hence laicism—is, in substance, produced by Christianity. In other words, Christianity is *the religion of the exit from religion*,[2] and democracy, the free market, civil rights, individual freedoms, and laicism have all been, if not precisely invented in the absolute sense, "facilitated" in their development and expression by the Christian cultures. Even Richard Rorty, a philosopher allergic to the religious, has recently conceded this—though without attempting an explanation of the historical reasons.[3]

CHRONICLE OF A DIALOGUE

As a matter of fact, the purpose of this book is twofold. As mentioned, the aim is first of all to supply the reader with some food for thought about problems that are at the center of recent theoretical and critical discussion, especially the relation between religion and modernity and the role of Christianity in a globalized and multicultural world, but also the complex and delicate interface between "truth" and "liberty," and "relativism" and "faith," and the dangers and tensions of a world in which new forms of religiously inspired violence have emerged. In addition, this volume aims to put on public record a philosophical rapprochement that has come about between two of the major contemporary European thinkers—the French anthropologist René Girard and the Italian philosopher Gianni Vattimo—in a series of dialogues that have taken place on various public and academic occasions and that are gathered here for the first time. Precisely because the aim is to create a record of an encounter and an open and friendly debate, free of polemical acrimony and imprinted with strong mutual respect, I have chosen to begin with three public debates between Girard and Vattimo and conclude with the more strictly philosophical articulation of their discussions, in the form of two essays in which they comment on each other's ideas, underlining the points of both convergence and dissent.

In this sense, more than a systematic treatise in philosophy or theology, this book could be defined as the "diary" of a meeting of minds prompted by the common willingness of the participants to engage in discussion and by a convergence of interests and philosophical questions. As regards the genesis and articulation of this dialogue, it should be emphasized that Vattimo was the first to engage all the ramifications of the themes treated here, primarily in books like *The End of Modernity* (1985), *The Transparent Society* (1989), *After Christianity* (2002), and *Nihilism and Emancipation* (2003).[4] Vattimo's principal aim over these years has been to rethink the philosophical perspectives put forward by Martin Heidegger and reshape them as a philosophy adequate to the fragmentation of meaning in which postmodern Western society finds itself immersed, a philosophy that could be used as a diagnostic instrument in this epochal transition, capable of constructing a horizon of expectations within which to make a series of political choices that would move in a progressive and emancipatory direction. In this philosophical and intellectual project, Vattimo has found a theoretical ally—not perhaps the most obvious one for those who have been following the evolution of Vattimo's ideas—in René Girard, a thinker who has, in contrast, made little use of his own anthropological theory to interpret contemporary social and political reality—both because he has never wished to assume the role of public thinker or militant intellectual (in the continental sense of the term "militant") like many of his French colleagues and also because he has always been more interested in the analysis of mythical cultures, on the one hand, and in the revelatory perspicacity of the Bible vis-à-vis the sacral violence of the natural religions, on the other. For all that, however, Girard has recently found himself inevitably dragged into a series of public debates as crucial historical events (religious terrorism *in primis*) have turned out to pertain to his own theoretical perspectives: few other thinkers over the last half century have thought through the relation between religion and violence as thoroughly as he has, starting with his fundamental text, *Violence and the Sacred* (1972).[5]

In this light, Vattimo deserves recognition for not letting prejudice prevent him from drawing close to an "untimely" and not especially "politically correct" author like Girard and for having begun to talk about the role and the importance of religion from within his own philosophical perspective well before recent headline-making events dramatically illustrated the urgency of rethinking the religious in contemporary terms. Evidence of this can be found in the third of the debates appearing in this book, which dates from 1996, and the two final essays, which both date from 1999.[6] Yet Vattimo remained faithful to his own deconstructive, hermeneutic, and relativistc stance, even in the wake of 9/11, when a whole swarm of intellectuals of various provenance were busy singing the *de profundis* of postmodernism and its philosophical variants. It should be clear, in other words, that in spite of the fact that these discussions are particularly salient for our present political and theoretical climate, the lines of thought found in this book are not the product of occasional or historically contingent solicitations; rather, they map a course of thought and intellectual research that has been developing over decades.

THE DEATH OF GOD

If we seek a unifying philosophical theme encompassing both authors, a common cornerstone of their outlook, that would be "the death of God" in both the philosophical and the anthropological senses, which Girard and Vattimo trace back to Nietzsche— whom Girard calls the greatest theologian of modern times.[7] This "death of God" is the fundamental theoretical premise for the whole of their shared discourse on the relation between Christianity and modernization. For both thinkers the "death of God" is to be understood as the exit from the religions of the sacred, and that exit comes about essentially through the Judeo-Christian tradition and, in particular, through Christ's revelation.

The vocabularies and the basic theoretical perspectives adopted by the two intellectuals are, however, quite different. From Vattimo's point of view, formed as it was by the texts of continental philosophers like Heidegger and Gadamer, the death of God proclaimed by Nietzsche should be understood in the Christian sense of the incarnation, as *kénosis*, that is, the weakening of the transcendental potency of the divine and its metaphysical essence. Historically, this weakening has produced the progressive destructuring and draining away of *all the ontological truths* that have characterized mankind's history and thought. According to Vattimo, the Christian God, incarnating himself and dying, put an end to the transcendental order, an end to the absolute and metaphysical potency of Being as understood in Platonic terms. Hence, for Vattimo, secularization

> comprises all the forms of dissolution of the sacred characteristic of the modern process of civilization. If it is the mode in which the weakening of Being realizes itself as the *kénosis* of God, which is the kernel of the history of salvation, secularization shall no longer be conceived of as abandonment of religion but as the paradoxical realization of Being's religious vocation.[8]

If one adopts an anthropological perspective, as Girard does, the demise proclaimed by Nietzsche (with an intuition that the German thinker did not fully articulate philosophically but that Girard discerns as subtext) refers rather to the recollection of the *real* death of an innocent victim. In his polemic against

Christianity, Nietzsche was able to discern the real anthropological kernel of religion: its sacrificial and victimizing origins. As *Things Hidden Since the Foundation of the World* argues in detail, for Girard all human culture has a systemic origin based on the sacrifice, spontaneous at first but later institutionalized, of innocent victims, who served "pharmacologically" to resolve the crises into which archaic societies periodically plunged—victims who, on account of their "curative" powers, were divinized (hence the symbolic ambivalence of all the archaic divinities, at once wicked and beneficial).[9] The nexus between religion and violence, which appears so striking to us today, comes about not because religions are intrinsically violent but rather because religion is above all a mode of knowledge about mankind's violence and the ways of keeping it in check, about the "homeopathic" use of violence in order to control violence (from which derives Girard's interpretation of the apparently cryptic passage in the Gospels about "Satan casting out Satan"). Out of this cognitive and ritual grounding in the natural religions the Judeo-Christian tradition arose and gradually laid bare the mechanism underneath the human order: the persecution of innocent victims, who are expelled, scapegoated, and victimized most intensely at moments of crisis, whether natural, social, political, or systemic in general. Christ's persecution and death is both the repetition and the cognitive revelation of this mechanism, which for millennia has been at the base of human sociability and institutions. For Girard, the Christian gospel (or, if one prefers, the New Testament) was the hermeneutic key that made it possible, in history, to reinterpret both mythology and the Hebrew scriptures (or the Old Testament) as the gradual emergence into historical awareness of the violent and persecutory matrix of the social and cultural order, and to interpret the sacrifice of Christ as the moment of rupture of the equilibrium that had kept the symbolic-religious mechanism on which the archaic societies were based stable, recurring, and mythical. In the Girardian understanding, adopted here by Vattimo as well, Christianity becomes the key moment of an anthropological development that sees mankind engaged in a never-ending struggle with the danger of contagious violence internal to the community. The only way to contain it is to hunt for—and find—new victims every time, fresh scapegoats who are believed guilty but are actually innocent. "It is better for one man to die for the people, than for the whole nation to be destroyed" (John 11:49–50) runs the sacrificial logic. What Christ does is to reveal, to bring right out into the open, the arbitrariness and the radical injustice of this persecution: "They hated me for no reason" (John 15:25).[10]

The theoretical and hermeneutic wager linking Vattimo's thinking to Girard's is based, therefore, on the realization that Christianity is not a "religion" in the strict sense but a principle that destructures all the archaic religions and must temporarily clothe itself as an institutional "religion," too, so as to be able to enter into dialogue with the historicity of religions. Like a Trojan horse, it penetrates the age-old citadel of the mentalities instituted by the natural religions and empties it *from inside*, adopting the language and symbolism of the religions but completely reversing their meaning, demystifying all the violence on which the walls of the citadel of the sacred had been erected. Christianity represents the moment at which it is suggested, or rather, revealed to mankind that it can free itself from the need to resort to scapegoats and their immolation as a system for ending conflicts and crises within communities. And that entails becoming aware of the innocence of all those victims sacrificed to that end and of the substantial arbitrariness and injustice of their persecution.

Precisely this death of God, Christ's death, which Christianity has posited as foundational and revelatory and which the Western cultural tradition has introjected and metabolized with all its consequences, is the basis of the cultural processes that have led to the Western world as we know it. The historical progression that has brought us here has, for sure, been contested and intermittent (modern history is still full of violence, victims, and unjust persecutions) and has met strong resistance and inertia of a socio-anthropological kind. But the result is a world driven by ethical principles according to which the rights and freedoms of every single individual have to be protected; in which all the world's victims are given succor and protection; and in which the separation of church and laic state is fully incorporated, not just given by history but openly prescribed by Christian doctrine. The latter explicitly provides room for the rationale of politics ("give back to Caesar what belongs to Caesar"), although it does not regard this rationale as sufficient for constructing the true peace of mankind.[11]

The rupture of the sacrificial circle, accomplished by the Judeo-Christian revelation (in Girard's terms) or the *kénosis* of God through the incarnation (in Vattimo's), launched a historical development that culminates in the present age. This is the extraordinary paradox of Western culture, which—at precisely the historical moment when, with modernity and postmodernity, it appears poised to free itself definitively from the constriction of religious and confessional bonds, through what Girard characterizes as a "rationalist expulsion of the religious"—reveals its profoundly Christian roots. Girard sees proof of this in the fact that the entire discursive and ideological horizon of contemporary culture turns around the centrality of the victim: the victims of the Shoah, the victims of capitalism, the victims of social injustice, of war, political persecution, ecological disaster, racial, sexual, and religious discrimination.[12] This perspective fits so naturally with our way of thinking that it is sometimes difficult for us to perceive it as the outcome of a particular historical process or to reflect on how much of this "ethical kernel" of our convictions as men and women of the modern West we owe to the religious tradition from which we come: the Judeo-Christian one, the tradition that places the victim at the center of its theological and anthropological discourse.

SECULARIZATION AND APOCALYPSE

Starting then from the premise that Christianity and secularization are closely connected, it might be interesting to focus more closely on the modalities of this process, from the historical point of view and with respect to its contemporary phenomenology. Although it is not possible here to supply a detailed reconstruction of such a vast and complex evolutionary course, the debate between Girard and Vattimo has thrown into relief a shared tendency to view the process of secularization, in respect to its extreme consequences, as an "end of history"—not in the sense in which Francis Fukuyama uses the term, obviously, but in the sense of thinking through the ultimate consequences of this process of the desacralization of the world propelled by Christianity. The positions of Girard and Vattimo reflect their different hopes and fears.

Gianni Vattimo's main preoccupation (and readers will note the urgency with which he advances it in these debates) remains, first, to elaborate a system of thought capable of shedding light on the process of the destructuring of all claims to define, in "natural," fixed terms, what human beings are, and all the "scientific," ontological "truths" posited about them. For Vattimo these are contingent products of history, and above all ideological superstructures that have been used as tools of coercive imposition on the part of those who, over the course of time, have held economic, political, or symbolic power. Second, Vattimo wishes to inscribe the hermeneutic philosophical tradition (Nietzsche, Gadamer, Heidegger, Derrida) to which he himself belongs in a "history of revelation," registering the linkage between "nihilist ontology and the *kénosis* of God," and showing that the interpretive freedom that we have acquired over the course of our cultural history is itself a sign of the process of weakening of Being begun by the Christian revelation. Into Vattimo's substantial relativism and the "weak" perspective of his thought, then, there paradoxically insinuates itself a teleological reading of the destiny of Christianity, which appears to be guided, through the operation of grace, by a historically linear and immanent finalism: the destiny of Christianity is to dissolve all the ontological and alethic structures that human beings have, with violence, imposed on other human beings, and all those coercive agencies that have limited, and continue to limit, individual freedom. The way will then be opened to a community of love or agape, based on the sharing of principles that will be negotiated on the basis of intersubjective agreement. For Vattimo, this is essentially "the Kingdom of God."

While Girard may see in this position a perspective he can theoretically share as a possible sociohistorical diagnosis of the modern age, his assessment is more guarded than that of Vattimo. He sees the latter's diagnosis as depending on a philosophical stance too closely tied to what has been called "the linguistic turn" and that has, for the same political reasons that drove that philosophical and critical project, effected a dissolution of the reality principle. Girard, on the contrary, starts from an anthropological perspective of an utterly realist kind and from what he calls "common knowledge," seeing mankind and history in a context of "evolutionary permanence." Without assigning them immutable characteristics (something Vattimo often imputes to him), Girard does emphasize forms of psychological, sociological, and anthropological "inertia," which impose a *longue durée* on the process of transforming these "persistences." In particular, it is the survival of persecutory mechanisms, albeit in ever more problematic and attenuated forms, that accounts for the recurrence of violence even in the Christian ages. Girard does not claim to ontologize phenomenal reality, but he does claim to discern a development that is advancing much more slowly and with more difficulty than any of us, including Vattimo, would wish and that is grounded both in the desiring and competitive tendencies of human beings and in the survival of social mechanisms of exclusion and persecution.

Girard therefore does not believe that postmodernity is the awareness, achieved by modern mankind, that it lives "without anxiety in the relative world of half-truths."[13] For him the "intersubjective linguistic consensus" that Vattimo hopes will be achieved in a community of charity, which will pacify itself through the practice of interpersonal dialogue, in a sharing of language and preferences, is in fact still too solipsistic because it does not articulate the modalities and dangers of its own internal relations. The latter are *mimetic*, meaning imitative and rivalrous, with the potential to turn antagonistic at any moment and erupt into violence. So while sharing many of Vattimo's theoretical premises, Girard sets brackets around his "faith" that the history of revelation has a "progressive," linear path, voicing his own apprehension that sooner or later there may occur historical convulsions for which he adopts the terms "tragedy" and "apocalypse." The latter is meant in the double sense it bears for the modern reader: apocalypse as "revelation" and as the "violent end of time."[14] The revelation of the Christian message, a message that ruptures the barriers imposed by the natural religions, may indeed guide mankind to salvation in the peace of God, but in the meantime it has also stripped mankind of those sacral protections that had been put in place to protect it against its own violence. Christianity is creatively liberating, but in this liberation there is also space for a negative creativity, diabolic and destructive. If the sacrificial mechanism can no longer function because its absolute injustice and arbitrariness have been revealed, then modern society finds itself in a new *experimental* phase in which history becomes a laboratory for finding new mechanisms of equilibrium and stability. Modern individualism, international and democratic institutions, and globalization itself are all factors that prove how the Christian comprehension of reality has expanded, forcing the abandonment of the sacred and the secularization of the world. But they also connote a historical phase in which mankind is no longer protected by the false transcendence of the sacred, by the rigid mechanisms of a mentality formed by the pharmacological use of systemic violence. So mankind needs to resort to different "containment" structures to forestall the apocalyptic event, ones based on secularized forms of transcendence or "false transcendence" (for instance, the ideology of the democratic state, technology, mass-media spectacle, the commodification of individual relations, etc.). Hence, according to Girard, it is necessary not to rush the dissolution of what Saint Paul, in his letter to the Thessalonians, defined as the *katechon*, meaning the structures that hold human violence in check, including political and ecclesiastical structures and all those forces "stemming from the inertia of the powers of this world."[15] Vattimo, for his part, rejects any apocalyptic perspective, foreseeing a progressive liberation, through the grace of God, from any need for limits of any sort, even of the instructively "catechetic" kind, including the church.

FOR A WEAK CHURCH?

The opposition that emerges between Vattimo and Girard is clearly not confined to method and language alone: it inevitably has a political dimension. In comparison to other dialogues on religion that Vattimo has had with such thinkers as Richard Rorty or Jacques Derrida, ideologically more akin to himself,[16] we observe a greater divergence or polarization in this dialogue and a different political agenda: Vattimo the "progressive" tries to drag Girard the "conservative" onto his own terrain, asking him to accept all the theoretical consequences implicit in his own analysis of Christianity as the religion that reveals the victimizing foundation of human culture; that destructures all the natural religions from within, steering them toward their own disappearance; that heralds the deconstruction of all the rigid structures imposed by history: state or ecclesiastical apparatuses, authoritarian notions about truth and nature, and so on. Vattimo's claims obviously foreground a dispute that is not just philosophical but existential, in the sense that his own personal intellectual history has taken the shape of an attempt at reconciliation between the Catholic religious background and tradition from which he himself comes, and to which he feels a cultural and moral debt, and the project of emancipation to which he dedicates his own political activity. The struggle to win acceptance for sexual difference is a central theme of that project,[17] and one of the main obstacles it encounters is theological resistance on the part of the Catholic Church, which has, in Vattimo's opinion, concentrated an excessive proportion of its own pastoral energy on matters like the exercise of sexuality that it ought not to be meddling with at all.[18]

On these particular issues Girard has never expressed himself or, we may suppose, tends to comply with the magisterium of the Roman Church.[19] In general terms, though, one needs to remember that Girard's mimetic theory eludes confinement within any system of binary political opposition because the character of his analysis leads to phenomenological explanations possessing a high degree of ambivalence, which disclose a complex vision of reality in which the terms "positive" or "negative," "right" or "left," "progressive" or "conservative," can never be used in an absolute and unproblematic manner. As regards the history of the Catholic Church and its role in the postmodern era, it may indeed be the case that it is moving in the "debilist" direction for which Vattimo hopes, but the idea that the ecclesiastical apparatus will engage in some sort of instantaneous "euthanasia" the moment it realizes that the true destiny of Christianity is to extinguish itself is quite unthinkable for Girard. Historically, too, Girard knows that a "weaker," less structured or less hierarchical church offers society no guarantees against swerves into violence: on the contrary. The breakaway

Protestant churches, with "lighter," more "secular" ecclesiastical apparatuses and a hermeneutically more "mature" approach to the biblical text, have often produced harsher, less charitable theologies and more radical visions of what the spirit of Christianity should be, with less openness to alterity and to the "syncretic" universalism that inspired Catholicism. The breakaways often take place in the name of a purer rather than a more attenuated truth. Moreover, the cultural context that best exemplifies the drift of the religious toward individualistic and "privatistic" forms is the United States, with its astronomical number of churches and sects, and it hasn't produced a society less violent internally. On the other hand, there is the risk, to which the Anglican Church, for example, is exposed, of gradually becoming totally diluted into civil society, generating no "friction," as it were, with the social and the political, and so becoming an ineffective institutional force in ethical terms.

The original Italian title of this book, *Truth or Weak Faith?*, consequently predicates an ambivalence that is probably a little stronger than these two forms, one more "attenuated" than the other, would appear to express. On the one hand, we have *truth* as the truth of the *victim*, the truth of the Christian revelation, which has become an ethical kernel in our modernity—so that, for Girard, it is possible to accept social relativism but not epistemic relativism because our ethical understanding of the world is always centered on the consequences of the sacrifice of Christ. On the other hand, we have *weak faith*, which, although it does respond to a legitimate demand for emancipation, as Vattimo intuits, may also become, in our postmodern world, a form of "dechristianized" Christianity. For a weak faith does in fact amount to an increasingly individual and unstructured faith, "made to measure" to suit the needs and expectations of the individual.

And while corresponding, no doubt, to legitimate existential interests, this weak faith often appears to be no more than a variant of or an adaptation to the differentiation among the array of consumer goods, of individual choices, with which modern capitalism and the free market have structured individual preferences, about which Vattimo himself has expressed reservations.

But in reality, even on these points, the divergences between the two still leave room for a possible rapprochement. Vattimo lays claim to a salvific fidelity to tradition, as the main resource toward which one may turn in order to give meaning to one's own continuity of thought and action. This tradition, as effective historical event, sets bounds to the interpretive fragmentation of absolute epistemic and cultural relativism, making the history of the West (in a kind of ethnocentric move) the center of gravity of any capacity for hermeneutic and therefore social emancipation. Girard, for his part, while agreeing that we have to live in a laic society in which the autonomy of the political in the public realm is absolutely inviolate (and agreeing with Vattimo's view that "Christianity . . . must present itself as a bearer of the idea of secularity for the sake of its specific authenticity"),[20] nevertheless believes in fidelity to the church, in his case to the Roman Catholic Church, as a strong symbolic bulwark against the pathological drifts of contemporary, "liquid" individualism and as an indispensable historical tool for containing the violence and the self-destructive urges of mankind, which are ever ready to erupt.

TOWARD AN INTERRELIGIOUS DIALOGUE

On this score, while Vattimo may believe in the progressive and liberatory dissolution of all ontologies as the positive and irreversible destiny of Western culture, contemporary mankind—globalized and interconnected and exposed to ever more massive levels of interdependence and alterity   seems for its part disinclined to be satisfied with the vacuum left by the disappearance of faiths and ideologies or by the dissolution of the onto-theology of traditional philosophy: hence the signs of a return to forms of "post-secular" orthodoxy, as Jürgen Habermas has recently noted.[21] The problem is that today, with the dissolution of any solid philosophical, political, ethical, or religious foundation, its place is taken by the caricatural version called *fundamentalism*, which, in fact, recuperates all the persecutory forms typical of the sacred. Paradoxically, it is precisely the Muslim fundamentalists who are the most perspicacious in intuiting the linkage between desacralization and Christianity: they oppose the West for being Christian, of course, but, above all, for being secularized—laic, pluralist, and relativist.[22] What Islamic integrism fears in Christian culture is not the evangelical message or the authority of the pope but precisely its laicity and its secularization, its power to destructure the traditional religious order. Yet when the varieties of fundamentalism transmute into antagonistic violence, they reveal how much they themselves are already the product of a tormented historical negotiation with secularization and modernity. When, instead of shutting itself up in its own self-sufficiency, fundamentalism engages in open conflict with Western pluralism, that is because it *already shares* the basic preoccupations and interests of its adversary. The violence cloaked in religion that Islamic extremists perpetrate is, in fact, already symptomatic of the onset of the decomposition of the religious, of the fact that the culture to which they belong, like the whole world's culture for that matter, is already infiltrated with secular laicism, technological rationality, economic utilitarianism, para-ideological mass-media propaganda. Thus in the end they take their stance against the West in terms of pure mimetic rivalry.[23] And as far as that goes, the same is true for those in the opposing camp who fight against Islamic radicalism in a sectarian and ideologically charged manner, ultimately mimicking its very attitudes and language.

Granted all this, the next item on the agenda, so to speak, is naturally: How are we to go about constructing and articulating the necessary interreligious dialogue that we so much require in the present historical moment, starting from the theoretical premises established by Girard and Vattimo? Obviously the theoretical implications and sociopolitical ramifications are so complex that they go far beyond the themes broached in these dialogues, which have more limited and introductory aims, but we can certainly highlight some salient points from which a discussion might be launched: for example, the idea that a surreptitious Christianization of the world is occurring, driven by the spread of the free market and technologically organized society, on the one hand, and laic, democratic institutions on the other. On that basis, the Western Christian world might be seen, in Vattimo's words, as recuperating "its universalizing function without any colonial, imperialist, or Eurocentric implications . . . by stressing its missionary implication as hospitality, and as the religious foundation (paradoxical as this might be) of the laity."[24] If there is any respect in which Christianity is historically important, indeed decisive, for Girard and Vattimo, it is precisely the question of laicity, where the heritage of the Judeo-Christian tradition can come to terms with the other religions. This it can do because it can address the other faiths without presenting itself as the religious standard to which they must conform, on an even playing field of dialogue. Yet there is always the awareness that the "other" cultures also tend "to see the very secularity of the political as a threat to their authenticity, and therefore take it less as a condition of liberty than as a negative limitation that must be overcome."[25]

For both Girard and Vattimo, the challenge is to search, in the various confessional and religious traditions, for nodes of common understanding that may lead toward a *diminution of violence* and conflict. As far as Vattimo is concerned, in any intercultural and interreligious dialogue, any principle of equality whatsoever must always take second place to a criterion of the progressive diminution of violence. Hence the hermeneutic perspective he advocates undoubtedly bears a great deal of significance, considering how central the problem of *interpretation* is in freeing the religious from all forms of literalist fixation on the sacred texts, in *historicizing* the content of these texts and stripping them of the persecutory praxis typical of the sacred. This would, not incidentally, open a doctrinal and political channel of contact with the kind of moderate Islam (one thinks of intellectuals like the Iranian Mohsen Kadivar) that is coming to grips with fundamental questions like respect for human rights and minorities, the emancipation of women, and the abolition of corporal punishment, and is doing so precisely on the basis of a renewed hermeneutic relation to tradition and scripture.

For Girard, however, the point is how to counterbalance this necessary hermeneutic emancipation of the world religions with a common adherence to a victimary perspective. Even the anti-essentialist stance adopted by the "linguistic turn" actually has a concrete nub of resistance, according to the French thinker, an *essential* element that remains historically *irreducible* and represents the absolute with which even Vattimo, without saying so explicitly, reckons: the victim. For Girard, all of Christian knowledge boils down to this central core, which no nihilistic thought can succeed in deconstructing: the victim as the center of Western ethical thought and of all our political and moral concerns, a victim to be protected, defended, guaranteed, emancipated. What the identitarian logic of politically correct postmodern discourse promotes as an "incommensurability" among the visions of the world, among the discourses and conceptual schemas proper to the various cultures of the globalized world, turns out to be permeated with a sacrificial residue. Precisely in the exercise of this "incommensurability" a principle of "exclusion" is activated: it is permissible to persecute and exclude the other in order to affirm one's own identity. From this perspective, the terrain of shared dialogue for Girard can only be a victimology that does not produce more victims, given that conflict between religions, or between ethnic groups, is often grounded in the ostentatious assumption of victim status in order to put the rival group at a disadvantage—in the claim to be more of a victim than the other side and so justify one's own retaliatory violence. This, from a Girardian point of view, is yet another proof of the substantial Christianization of the symbolic vocabulary of the international community (in other words, a horizontal comprehension, operating interculturally and interreligiously, of the mechanism of victimization), but one that risks being turned around and directed back at Christianity, as an instrument of reprisal.

For Girard the basic aim should be to recognize and recuperate the "prophetic" dimension present in all religions, to the extent that all have contributed, following different historical paths and trajectories, to the slow revelation of the truth of victimhood, a truth that, while it is set forth in complete form in Christianity, does not monopolistically belong to it, or to the Catholic Church, or to the West, but to humanity in its entirety.[26]

1 | CHRISTIANITY AND MODERNITY

Gianni Vattimo and René Girard

PIERPAOLO ANTONELLO: I would like to begin our dialogue with the two terms that supply the framework for this encounter: Christianity and modernity. Your conceptual instruments are different—anthropological for Girard, philosophical for Vattimo—but you wind up saying more or less the same thing: that modernity, as constructed and understood by the European West, is substantially an invention of Christianity. Your research has led you to the apparently paradoxical result that Christianity is responsible for the secularization of the world. The end of the religions was brought about by a religion. In a recent book, Girard actually informs us that "in its modern acceptation, *atheism is a Christian invention*."[1] Hence it is a historical and philosophical error from your vantage point to regard secularization and laicity, as these terms are commonly understood, as being opposed to, and in conflict with, Christianity. How can we explain this apparent paradox?

RENÉ GIRARD: To articulate the reasons for this from my point of view, we have to start from an anthropological and historico-evolutionary perspective. I link secularization and Christianity essentially because Christianity caused a break in the cultural history of mankind, in particular the history of mankind's religions, which for tens of thousands of years had allowed primitive communities to avoid self-destructing. Human beings are often violent, in fact, more violent than animals. But this violence has to be clearly understood. When I speak of violence, I don't mean aggression; violence is something I consider inherent in social dynamics, where it occurs in the form of reprisal, vendetta, the urge to take an eye for an eye and a tooth for a tooth. The reason is that human beings are inherently competitive and, as I call them, "mimetic": they always desire the same things others do, and they tend toward a type of conflict that is internal, reciprocal, and potentially never ending, giving rise to vicious circles of violence that, prior to the institution of judicial systems, only religion, with its norms, rituals, and taboos, had the capacity to confine. Myths, especially myths of origin, always begin by recounting a crisis in human relations, which often takes the guise of an "affliction" or "plague." This crisis is normally resolved through a dramatic alteration in the mimetic unanimity: the violence of the community, collective violence, all devolves onto a single victim, a victim chosen for arbitrary reasons. The killing of this victim reestablishes the social order. So precious and fruitful is the latter that the community is led to invest the very victim it has expelled with sacral power, divinizing it. "To sacrifice" in fact means "to make sacred." In broad outline, this is the mythical structure of the primitive cultures and religions, the foundational act of which is the lynching or the expulsion, real at first, and later symbolic, of an innocent victim.

What Christianity does is to depart from this primitive mindset—because, contrary to what anthropologists have often maintained, Christianity is not a myth like all the others—by completely reversing the perspective. In myth, the standpoint is always that of the violent community that discharges its violence onto a victim it sees as guilty and whom it expels as a means of reestablishing the social order. In the mythic account the victim is always guilty, and is represented as such. Think of Oedipus, who commits parricide and incest and for that is expelled from the city. Freud takes this myth at face value, believing that what it represents is true, whereas Christianity helps us to understand the hidden and repressed truth. Myth in the natural religions stages a masquerade of sorts, and the crowds, gripped by the mimetic paroxysm, believe in it; they remain "ignorant" precisely because, as the gospel says, "they know not what they do" when they are subject to the mimetic frenzy. From the sociological and anthropological point of view, Christianity denies this mythic order, this mythical interpretation, because it recounts the same scene, but from the point of view of the victim, who is always innocent. Hence Christianity is destructive of the type of religion that brings people together, joining them into a coalition against some arbitrary victim, as all the natural religions have always done, except for the biblical ones.

Christianity reverses this situation, demonstrating that the victim is not guilty and that the unanimous crowd knows not what it does when it unjustly accuses this victim. Examples can already be found in the Old Testament, prior to Christ's Passion, which for me represents the revelatory culmination of the innocence of the victim sacrificed by an unjust and violent community. Take the case of Isaiah 52–53, where it is evident that the victim is innocent but is condemned just the same by the crowd in the grip of the mimetic contagion, in other words, in the unanimous conviction that it has detected the one guilty of having caused all its own internal crises. In these circumstances we do not have individual behavior or conscience, only the unanimous logic of the crowd. Even Peter gives in to this temptation during the Passion, when he finds himself in the midst of the mob accusing Christ and denies him. With the gospel and the Passion of Jesus, this anthropological truth about humanity is revealed, put on display in its entirety: we, in our history as cultural animals, have always sought scapegoats in order to resolve our crises, and we have killed and then divinized them without knowing what we were doing. Christ's Passion shows us what we were doing and does so in stark terms: Jesus is an innocent victim sacrificed by a crowd that turns unanimously against him after having exalted him only a few days before—and for no particular reason. Awareness of this kind causes the mechanism of misrecognition and cognitive concealment that underlay the mythical schema to fracture. Henceforth we can no longer pretend not to know that the social order is built upon the blood of innocent victims. Christianity deprives us of the mechanism that formed the basis of the archaic social and religious order, ushering in a new phase in the history of mankind that we may legitimately call "modern." All the conquests of modernity begin there, as far as I am concerned, from that acquisition of awareness within Christianity.

ANTONELLO: Gianni Vattimo, your perspective incorporates Girard's premises, especially as they are set out in *Things Hidden Since the Foundation of the World*, but gives them a different, philosophical declension, integrating them into Heidegger's thinking on the end of metaphysics and the dissolution of Being, meaning of any ontologically stable truth. Through the incarnation and death of Christ, and the consequent revelation of the violent mechanism of victimhood that underlay the sacred and the natural religions, we learn that it is actually God who "weakens himself," opening a space in which mankind may achieve emancipation, to the point of actually being able to become "laic" and "atheist."

GIANNI VATTIMO: First of all, I ought to state that René Girard has helped to inspire my own conversion—although I'm not sure how pleased he would be to find out what he has converted me into! Reading Girard's work was as decisive for me as it was to read some of the works of Heidegger, which left a profound mark on me in a different period of my life, and not just in intellectual terms but existential and personal ones too. Girard made it possible for me to grasp the historical-progressive essence of Christianity and modernity, the meaning of their eventuation. All of us who were raised in Catholic cultures normally assume that there is an antithesis and an opposition between being Christian and being modern. The French Revolution, the thinkers of the Enlightenment, democracy, liberalism, all the "errors" condemned in the papal *Syllabus* of 1864—for those who have read it—were conceived in opposition to religious faith, and Christianity in particular, which was seen as conservative and obscurantist. Modernity was one thing and Christianity something else. In philosophy, to be Christian one had to turn back to philosophers of the past, Aristotle, Saint Augustine, Saint Thomas Aquinas, and so on.

Discovering Girard meant discovering that Jesus came to disclose something the natural religions had failed to reveal. He disclosed the victimary mechanism on which they were founded—a revelation that enabled us to undermine and finally dissolve a number of beliefs that were proper to the natural religions. The very history of Christianity is the history of the dissolution (assisted, I am Catholic enough to believe, by the Holy Spirit) of the natural-violent and natural-sacred elements that the church had retained. All the disciplines the Christians imposed on themselves in the tradition have something violent, but they are also linked to an imposition that has, in some manner, secularized itself. The key term that I began using after having read Girard is just that: *secularization*, which I take to mean the effective realization of Christianity as a nonsacrificial religion. And I carry this line of thought further because I see many of the apparently scandalous and "dissolute" phenomena of modernity as positive. In this light, secularization is not the relinquishment of the sacred but the complete application of the sacred tradition to given human phenomena. The example that springs to mind is Max Weber, who sees the birth of capitalist society as the legitimate offspring of the Protestant spirit. So in this sense I have a positive theory of secularization, one that originates from a reinterpretation of scripture by the church in which there is no victimhood. Ultimately, Christianity is the religion that opens the way to an existence not strictly religious, if we take "religious" to mean binding restraints, imposition, authority—and here I might refer to Joachim of Fiore, who spoke of a third age of the history of humanity and the history of salvation, in which the "spiritual" sense of scripture increasingly emerges and charity takes the place of discipline.

Starting from these premises, which as I say I derived from reading *Things Hidden*, I would however put the following question to Girard: hasn't Christianity introduced into the world something that really ought to consume the ecclesiastical apparatus, too? There is a dynamic element in the Christian revelation that said, "Look, the victim mechanism of the religions is horrible, and we must change it." But how far do we go with that? To what extent must Christianity consume all the elements of violence that there are in the religious traditions? If Catholic orthodoxy declares that no one may have an abortion, no one may divorce, there can't be experiments on embryonic stem cells, and so on, is this not the persistence of a certain violence belonging to natural religion within the framework of a historical-positive religion that revealed nothing except love? Jesus Christ came into the world in order to reveal that religiosity consists not in sacrificing but in loving God and our neighbor. All the things in the Church that don't boil down to this, aren't they still forms of natural victim religion?

ANTONELLO: René Girard, how do you respond to this objection? And what is the relationship between historical Christianity and the "sacred" heritage that the gospel of Jesus tries to supersede?

GIRARD: Gianni Vattimo is highly intelligent and simpatico, and I have great esteem for his ideas. What he has tried to suggest to you is that I approve everything the Church is, and has done, in the world. I do not maintain that Christianity has transformed the world to the extent it ought to or could have done. Christianity fought against the archaic religions, and it still struggles against more or less explicit forms of the sacred. Historical Christianity has maintained elements of archaic religion, of historical religion, and given that society, politics, culture, and the whole world in which we live are historical, the same thing holds true for the religions. There has been and there still is an attempt at adaptation, at adjustment, but obviously that requires a great deal of time because the Christian idea came into a world in which territoriality was strong, the concept of vendetta was strong, and the actions of human beings were highly constrained by the actions of groups, by mechanisms of unanimity that we may call tribal. The Christianity that tries to enter into this world, which is a world of perils, does not have an easy time;

clearly, it takes thousands of years of effort before it is able to break certain things down. This is what Vattimo doesn't see—or perhaps he is less obsessed than I am.

We know that we are living in a world in which the possibilities and the potentials for action on the part of mankind are constantly expanding, with ever more far-reaching repercussions. Primitive man often did not even dare to cultivate a particular piece of ground on account of the respect and fear with which the spirits that occupied it filled him (all those divinities that permeated nature and that, in my opinion, were originally scapegoats transformed into gods), whereas we no longer feel that sort of fear.

I agree with the view that the Enlightenment was a historical turning point, when the Christian and Western portion of humanity realized that the world was changing, that people were more free, that there was greater scope for action on the part of mankind, on account of the fact that the world was becoming desacralized in comparison with circumstances in pre-Christian times, or even just in the Middle Ages. But the erroneous belief took hold that this was only the upshot of the actions of men, of individual geniuses or the genius of the human species in general. At the same time, though, there was no corresponding growth in awareness of human responsibility in the world. We have ever more powerful weapons, but conversely we have very little sense of responsibility. If our cultural evolution has led us to substitute ourselves for God, then we had better realize that we have taken on an enormous responsibility, and we ought to be asking ourselves what the importance of religion is in an entirely different manner than that adopted by the communications media at the present time. From the perspective of the mass media, religion is seen as a mode of thought alien to human nature, a something-or-other that arrives as constriction, as impediment, as something that might be bad for your health: religion is as harmful to mankind as tobacco. But this discourse overlooks the fact that religion forms part of human nature, that having religious beliefs is in human nature, and on that basis religion cannot fail to have an anthropological and social purview. Today we are obliged to ask ourselves what it means to live in a world in which it is claimed that we can do without religion. Is there not danger in this, especially the danger of an eruption of violence? In a world in which, as we know, we are moving in a direction that could actually lead to the end of the world as we know it, doesn't the disappearance of religion expose us to the risk of finding ourselves in an "apocalyptic" dimension? Obviously what I am saying is incompatible with the apocalyptic mode of fundamentalist Protestantism, which foresees the destruction of the world by the violence of God, because that mode is essentially anti-Christian. In my view the truly apocalyptic texts, which unfortunately are seldom cited, are chapter 13 of the gospel of Mark, and chapter 24 of Matthew, which, from the viewpoint of fundamental Christianity, I regard as even more important than the Johannine Apocalypse.

And yet, knowing what is at stake, we make a joke out of biblical texts like the Apocalypse when we ought to be taking them seriously, seeing that in the Apocalypse the end of the world is linked specifically to Christianity. Because Judaism and Christianity are aware that if we try to do away with all the prohibitions, the limits that the archaic religions imposed, we are putting at risk not only ourselves but the existence of the whole world. It was from this awareness that the archaic religions arose, in fact. We today, on the other hand, conduct ourselves as though we were the masters of the world, the lords of nature, with no mediation or arbitration, as though nothing we are doing could have negative repercussions. But we all know perfectly well that these archaic taboos had force and significance. Neither human beings nor nations can live without an ethic. It is pleasing to imagine and profess that anything is possible, but in reality every one of us knows that there are limits. If human beings and nations continue to evade these responsibilities, the risks will become enormous. Vattimo would have us believe that we might be able to live in some sort of Eden if we simply realized that we were already there, if we realized that these dangers do not exist, but unfortunately the world around us pays him no heed.

We are in need of a good theory of secularization because secularization also entails the end of the sacrificial, and that is a development that deprives us of the ordinary cultural equipment for facing up to violence. There is a temporality to the sacrificial, and violence is subject to erosion and entropy, but Vattimo's approach seems to me to combat its symptoms. When, thanks to Christianity, we get rid of the sacred, there is a salvific opening up to *agape*, to charity, but there is also an opening up to perhaps greater violence. We are living in a world in which we know that there is less violence than in the past, and we take care of the victims in a way that no other civilization has ever known, but we are also the world that persecutes and kills more people than ever. The world we are living in gives the impression that both good and evil are on the rise. And if one has a theory of culture, he or she must account for the extraordinary aspects of this culture. In his book *Belief*, Vattimo uses Max Weber's view of secularization as the source of the disenchantment of the world. You say that "disenchantment has also produced a radical disenchantment with the idea of disenchantment itself."[2]

I agree. For all his intelligence, Weber only went part way in bringing to light this paradoxical process, represented as it is by the contemporaneous presence of great development and a high degree of disintegration. But it has many other aspects that are intensifying with the passage of time and growing ever more fascinating as they do so.

VATTIMO: I may have oversimplified Girard's thought in my opening statement. I certainly do not understand him as someone who wants to impose a freeze, and I didn't mean to make him more papist than he may appear to be. In him, even in what he has just stated, one feels the presence of an idea of human nature as something that, in some manner, sets limits. I, in contrast, am convinced that, following the same path, one could also deconstruct the limit-setting conception of human nature. Gianni Baget Bozzo would say that Jesus took human form so he could explain to us that the devil exists and poses real danger.[3] But then, he could have sent us a letter, and avoided getting himself crucified! Christians of a different stamp than Baget Bozzo might say that Jesus took human form not just to reveal that evil exists but also in order to destroy it. He didn't come to tell us, "Remember that you will die," but rather to proclaim, "Death, where is your victory?"

With Girard's theory as a point of departure, it is possible to really elaborate a discourse on Christianity that doesn't describe "true" human nature but *changes* it, redeems it. Redemption lies not just in knowing that God exists but in knowing that God loves us and that we need have no fear of the darkness. How far down this road can we push ourselves? My objection to Girard, and my own idea, is that with Christianity we can truly say, "Thanks to God, I'm an atheist"; in other words, thanks to God I'm not an idolater, thanks to God I don't believe that there are laws of nature, I don't believe there are markers beyond which we cannot go. I believe only that I ought to love God above all else and my neighbor as myself.

A conservative Catholic might ask me: "But when you say you love God, what is it you love? Shouldn't you be saying that you love the laws of nature?" The answer is no, because this identification of God with laws of nature is extremely dangerous. On that basis, I would also have to love the fact that whites have traditionally been richer, had a different social status, than blacks. The laws of the market tell us that the strong are winners and the weak are losers. Laws of nature like that are the kind that are preached by the right! That is why I am not a naturalist, in any sense. Certainly, the world was created by God, but how literally do I have to take that? If God arranged for the big fish to eat the little fish, does that mean I have to supply the big fish with sardines and anchovies, aid them just because the law of nature dictates I should? Or should I try to change them, make them into vegetarians for example? Does it violate the laws of nature to transform a carnivore into a herbivore? That seems to me absurd. But it would be a Christian truth in Girard's sense. It is true that Girard is more of an anthropologist than a philosopher, as Antonello said at the outset, and that at the base of his thinking, as we see in the book *Evolution and Conversion*, there is still the idea that the laying-bare of the victim mechanism, which Jesus made possible by offering his life, is a key to understanding human nature and describing it more adequately. But I don't go along with that because I learned from Heidegger and Nietzsche that any erecting of structures whatsoever is always an act of authority. Who is it that asks to see your identity card? The police. So why is it so hard to bring Girard to the point of conceding that there is a dynamic and revelatory essence in

Christianity and that the goal of history and the purpose of life are to knock down ever more barriers? Hegel believed that, and so did the Enlightenment. We can't accept that there are limits signposted "ne plus ultra." Jesus came to tell us that *nothing* is impossible.

Of course I don't believe we're in Eden. But there are moments of fulfillment when we do love, and those could be made more lasting if we could all manage to live with a bit more love for one another—not an impossible circumstance, given that human nature doesn't have these limits. "You must therefore be perfect just as your heavenly Father is perfect." That's from the gospel of Matthew (5:48). I desire to be perfect, like my Father. Could Jesus possibly have commanded us to do something absolutely impossible?

ANTONELLO: But wouldn't you agree nevertheless that, as Girard maintains, we live within a historical dimension, which means that humans in every society must impose ordinances on themselves, limits of an ethical sort? Not the system of taboos and prohibitions of the sacred, of the pretechnological societies, of course, but normative "structures" of shared behavior. And what role does Christianity have to play in constructing this common ethic?

VATTIMO: What I primarily believe is that Girard's discourse should be taken up and interpreted in the sense of a self-consuming dynamic within Christianity.[4] Ever fewer idols, ever more "atheism." No natural proofs of God, only charity and, of course, ethics. I always say that ethics is merely charity plus the traffic regulations. I respect the rules of the road because I don't want to cause the death of my neighbor and because I ought to love him. But to suppose that there is something about running a red light that goes against nature is ridiculous. If you think about ethics in a Christian light, that's all it is: charity plus the traffic rules. Otherwise you are always going to come up against someone who tells you that he knows the natural laws better than you do. Some might ask me: "So what do *you* believe in?" I am a democratic citizen, the only things I am obliged to save are my soul and my liberty. My liberty signifies being informed, giving my consent, making laws on which we all agree, showing each other mutual respect in the name of charity. I know it isn't easy, but all the other mechanisms have always led to the existence of authorities who knew what I ought to be doing better than I did and so imposed something on me.

I bear responsibilities toward others and therefore toward the history of the church, toward humanity, too. I have no wish to behave like a bull in a china shop, wrecking the whole place. For the Christian saints I have great respect. I once said that I would sooner resemble Saint Joseph, with his air of being the "putative" father of his child, than an iron-jawed figure like the business leader Cesare Romiti.[5] I have great respect for the Christian tradition, for sainthood, but not to the point of not taking a bath so as to avoid seeing my own naked body, as San Luigi Gonzaga is said to have done. He did so because he was a saint; I prefer not to go around smelling bad. All this is just charity plus the traffic rules: ethics is just that.

GIRARD: I have no objection to most of what Vattimo has said. In the intellectual life of Europe, his conversion back to Catholicism was an important event because he belongs, or belonged, to the current that moved through Heidegger to structuralism and then on to deconstruction. And this current is characterized by an attitude of extreme optimism about history. For them history doesn't really mean a lot. The key term for defining this school could be "game." Everything is ludic; it's a linguistic game. From a sociological point of view, they are allowed, you might say, since the majority of the exponents of this school come from the academy and are convinced that there will always be a university to sustain them, with constant financial support flowing from the capitalist system, that no problems will intrude from outside. They won't earn the salaries earned by the engineers of Silicon Valley, but their lives are nevertheless fairly easy and smoothly functioning.

This school set out to break with German idealism but not to deconstruct our civilization or our world. And the manner in which Vattimo has reacted to this type of stance is admirable. In this connection, it is becoming clearer all the time that religion defeats philosophy and outstrips it. In fact, the various philosophies are practically dead on their feet; the ideologies are virtually defunct; political theories are almost at an end; and faith in science as a substitute for religion is by now a hollow faith indeed. There is a new felt need for religion, in some form. And Vattimo realized this. But there are a few aspects of his thought in which that ludic atmosphere of the school in which he originated, and from which he has taken his distance, still persist a bit too much for my taste.

I believe we are living in a world in which tragedy is reemerging at all levels—political, ecological, and social. It is easy for us to be living in a world as well organized as the Western world. But we are part of the privileged 25 percent of the world population. There are problems that are no longer internal to any particular society, that are planet-wide, especially when we take into account that only one-third or one-quarter of the world population can possibly approach the kinds of privilege we have. If our world is one to which tragedy is making a return, and if we start to see this tragedy as a religious tragedy, then there is hope. If we consider it as a Greek tragedy, on the other hand, then we are finished.

VATTIMO: Just as I exaggerated Girard's traits at the outset, now he's painting me as a fun-seeking gamester. Indeed it's true that I don't take myself as seriously as other Italian philosophers, and perhaps I ought to behave a little more solemnly. In reality I am well aware of the ills that beset us. And it's true that I tend not to see these ills as a sign of human nature but as a sign of the wickedness of some, of the class struggle, of authoritarianism, things like that.

Quite right, we can no longer take Greek tragedy seriously because when Oedipus killed that wretch Laius and wed Jocasta, he didn't know they were his parents. As the Enlightenment thinkers would say, he was in ignorance, ruled by his destiny. But if everyone had been carrying an identity card with their name and address, things would have been cleared up immediately. To take facetiousness to the limit, you could say that in Greek tragedy the absence of a registry office for vital records created problems!

I am by no means convinced that we live in the best of all possible worlds. And as far as that goes, I might counter by asking whether that is a consequence of the fact that we were too busy seeking amusement in games, or the fact that we were too serious. Sergio Quinzio wrote thunderous tracts in which he maintained that Christianity is a failure because look where we are after having been acquainted with it for 2000 years.[6] But is this properly the fault of the amusement seekers, or of the tradition that is what it is? And might it not be a good idea, consequently, to stake out a position a bit less naturalistic, authoritarian, boundary-setting, and metaphysical? Spirit [*spirito*] could finally just be spirited wit [*la battuta di spirito*], instead of all that cumbrous discourse. Paradise can't be anything but play. The goal of our lives is aesthetic rather than ethical, even if ethics counts for a great deal in the meantime. And when I say "in the meantime," I am talking about respect for others rather than respect for objective norms.

I even view the trajectory of contemporary philosophy— from Wittgenstein's language games to the idea of Being as event in Heidegger to Richard Rorty's particular version of pragmatism—as a passage from *veritas* to *caritas*. In other words truth matters nothing to me except in relation to some particular goal. Why study chemistry? Because I can construct things that are of use to me and my neighbor. But frankly, knowing that 2 plus 2 makes 4 does nothing per se to bring me closer to God, any more than it would to believe that 2 plus 2 makes 220. Otherwise everything would be a handbook of geometry! But the Bible isn't a handbook of astronomy or cosmology, it isn't even a handbook of theology. It may say that God is father; today nobody is scandalized anymore if we also call God mother, uncle, or near relative. Why on earth ought we to think of him as a father?

I, too, am convinced that, as Girard said, there is a return to religion today because people have realized that all the forms of knowledge regarded as definitive have turned out to be dependent on historical paradigms, on various kinds of conditioning— social, political, ideological, and so on. No longer can we assert that since science knows nothing of God, God does not exist. Science isn't even able to establish if it means anything to say that I am in love. All the essential things that characterize our lives, like feelings, values, hopes, are not objects of science.

So it doesn't scandalize me in the least that God is not an object of science; indeed, if anything it is one more reason to believe in him rather than to get rid of him. "Only a God can save us," Heidegger said. But which God? The God of natural theology, of fixed laws, of insuperable boundaries? God the judge who'll be certain to take pleasure when I am in hell because I've been a bit wicked? Do you really believe in that? Well, if that's God, you can keep him! That is precisely the god that Jesus intended to deny when he said, "I shall not call you servants any more . . . I call you friends" (John 15:15), and, "You will be with me in my kingdom."

ANTONELLO: In this process of "self-consumption" of ontological truths, what stance ought we to adopt vis-à-vis the historical tradition, upon which we always draw, and which is characterized in any case by a faith in these "truths"? Moreover, on the basis of what shared theological or moral premises will it be possible to construct an interreligious dialogue, seeing that other traditions will probably have a hard time accepting Western philosophical nihilism, not to speak of its materialist and secular offshoots?

VATTIMO: An Anglican lady said to me once, "Do you realize that we are separated merely because Henry VIII remarried? Can we possibly still have these fixations?" When the pope meets the Dalai Lama, is he worried that the poor fellow will go to hell because he is not Catholic? Bergson makes an interesting remark somewhere to the effect that religions reach a mystical stage, and perhaps we will get to that mystical stage. Perhaps we might actually arrive at such a common dimension, but what impedes us is the same as the problem that afflicts the Italian left. And that is the fact that there are bureaucracies that do not want to give up their privileges. It's a bit like that with the churches. I see them as no more than officialdoms, which probably have their own reasons for thinking that women cannot become priests. Does charity have anything to do with the fact that women cannot become priests? No. What then? It is just a question of historical circumstance. In the time of Jesus women weren't lawyers or engineers, but neither were the apostles Poles (or Germans). They were however married men, fishermen, and tax collectors: the pope, however, is not a married man, nor has he ever plied the trade of fisherman.

I mean, even from the ecumenical point of view, it would promote interfaith dialogue if we put a bit of distance between ourselves and these political officialdoms. When Cardinal Ruini states that the crucifix is the symbol of Italian nationality, I'd reach down from the cross and cuff him if I were Jesus. For heaven's sake! I don't want Jesus made into a supporter of the Northern League; he has nothing to do with our nation.[7] Perhaps not even with the identity of Europe. Or rather: precisely as a Christian, I believe that we should not make the question of the "Christian roots" of the European Union a focus of opposition, a theme of conflict. If that's how things are, better not to talk about it.

In debate I exaggerate the polemical thrust of the things I am saying, but I do believe that if ethics has any inherent validity, it lies in keeping faith with those who came before me and with those who will come after—and so with the history and traditions of the saints, too. I can't discard them because they are all I have. They are the rigging of this vessel, like the Holy Scripture and the teachings of the Catholic Church. To me these are like the torch in a relay race that I have to carry for a while and hand over to those who will follow on. I can't withhold it or bury it, like the talents in the parable.

This might be a good project for Christianity, I think. What project can I have in the world if I am a Christian? To defend the authority of the church and its dogmas, or to strive for a different situation, an ecumenical situation, a situation in which we really come together and feel mutual affection, even politically? I know it isn't easy, but the other path, the path of absolute certainties, has yielded the world we have now. Someone might object: "So then you are ready to liquidate all absolute certainties?" My answer is forthright: it's absolute certainties that have got us where we are now, speaking of tragedies. So let's get rid of them altogether, these truths!

GIRARD: I believe Vattimo is perfect just as he is, and I'm certainly not trying to moralize him or give him advice of any kind. But even from an aesthetic perspective, it's hard for me to accept his stance of no setting of limits, which as far as I am concerned really tends towards a refusal of ethics, in particular when we think about modernity and about what is set to be our near-term future. The refusal of ethics is one of the great clichés of modernity, and its sources lie in the eighteenth century or even earlier. But today its force is spent, in my opinion—even its aesthetic force.

I don't want to compel anyone to turn apocalyptic or sprinkle her head with ashes, but I have children and grandchildren, and I have to admit I am fearful. I have the sensation that something increasingly frightful is occurring in our world. I began to think about what was in store for the world in 1945, when the atomic bomb was invented and used. To this point the atomic bomb has not been as destructive as we may have feared because the power of dissuasion worked. Toward the middle of the 1950s we realized that the Russians no doubt had many defects but that they certainly didn't want to die. But in today's world we see that increasing numbers of people are prepared to die in order to kill innocent parties whom they have never seen before. If we find ourselves facing terrorism that has managed to defeat and neutralize even the most sophisticated and efficient technologies, then we have to realize that we have entered a world open to possibilities that didn't exist before, possibilities especially frightening to us, belonging as we do to the privileged part of the world. For me, all this demands some deep reflection, of a kind that seems to be missing from today's political debate.

I would like to add something with respect to the problem of truth, as raised by Vattimo. I am religious, but why? In my opinion it all relates to the "revelation of the victim mechanism." For me this "revelation" corresponds to the Passion. Why does Christianity lay so much emphasis on the Passion? The Passion is described as the death of our Savior, and that is important not just from a religious point of view but also from an anthropological one, since it supplies us with a perspective on the other side of human culture. Every myth is a failed Passion. Not in the sense that the victim was not killed, but that the anthropological truth of this death, of this innocent death, was not unveiled. The question the Passion poses is: which side are we on? Are we with the crowd that accuses Jesus of being guilty, or are we on the other side?

In my view the superior revelatory force of the Passion in comparison to the Old Testament is that it is didactic in a very practical way. Not only does it show us the *truth* that was proper to all the previous myths, it makes us see both positions at the same time, one alongside the other. And that, I maintain, is an extraordinary thing. The Passion becomes the key to the understanding of mythology. Myth is always dominated by the viewpoint of the crowd, which designates the victim and proclaims his guilt, whereas in the Passion story we see the other side too, the position of the innocent victim. Now the question is, and this also applies to what Vattimo was saying: is all this *true* or *false*? If it is true, we are dealing with an *obvious*, self-evident truth. It is principally in these terms that I speak of "truth."

Some say I mix religion and science. It's not true. What I do say is that the argument I develop is overarching. Is Christianity really the opposing face of mythology? Is Christianity the truth of all mythology? All my thinking revolves around the question of whether Christianity isn't that which reveals the other side to us, the hidden side of myth. And by that I don't mean that it tells us the truth about God from the scientific point of view but that it tells us a truth about myth and about all of human culture. It's what American logicians call "common knowledge," it's common sense. And I believe we are moving toward a future where there will be ever greater acceptance of this common knowledge as part of our shared apprehension and that we will be living in a world that will be, and appear, just as Christian as it appears scientific to us today. I believe that we are on the eve of a revolution in our culture going beyond all expectation and that the world is headed for a change in comparison to which the Renaissance will dwindle to nothing. And obviously this is a fascinating prospect from my point of view.

VATTIMO: What Girard has said appears to me significant and surprising. In a certain sense, he seems to have become more optimistic than me. He appears to discern a Christian kernel in modernity that official Christianity has balked at acknowledging. For example, in my eyes the French Revolution was more Christian than the conservative-clerical reaction against it. From this standpoint, I, too, have faith that Christianity has been working away within Western civilization, coinciding with secularization, the discovery of political freedoms, and so on. Take the example of the globalization of information: we see tragedies like the one in Rwanda on television, and we grow anaesthetized. They don't concern us because we ourselves are doing quite nicely, thank you. Up to a point this is true, but I am also convinced that a little bit of everyday humanitarianism is being diffused throughout the world as well. People are doing unpaid work for charities in Italy and all over the world and adopting children from distant lands. I don't see that Western Christian culture is any worse than other cultures.

The future certainly scares me too, but more for ecological reasons than questions of good and evil. It's not natural for the world to end, any more than it's natural for 15 percent of humanity to consume 85 percent of the resources. Will we succeed, through discovering the truth of the victim mechanism, in becoming a civilization that doesn't limit itself to defending its own privileges? I am in agreement with what Girard has to say, but I'd also like to emphasize the importance of what he isn't saying. Does it make much sense, for example, to claim that a cognizance of the truth of the victim mechanism comparable to the cognizance of science is spreading? Wouldn't it be better instead if the cultures with roots in Christianity got better acquainted with the core of Christianity, rather than understanding it as an explanation that human nature is just what it is? Because in the latter case, let's just take up arms and get ready to defend ourselves at this point. If they attack you, what are you going to do, fall to your knees and pray? No, you set about changing politics, changing the political structures in such a way as to reduce violence. I agree with Girard's view that at the origin of history lie acts of violence. I am not entirely convinced that violence and killing amount to the same thing because I am a defender of euthanasia, for example. Violence for me is rather an act of imposition on the other and her liberty. If someone wants to throw herself out of the window, I will grab hold of her, and I may even restrain her for a few days. I will show her some tenderness, spend weeks talking to her. If she still wants to throw herself out the window following this therapy, I have to let her go ahead because her freedom is more important than her immediate viability and her survival. Here is an interesting question for debate: Isn't violence exemplified in the authoritarianism that says, "This is how you have to think, period"? Is Christianity not rather an act of love than a revelation of truth? It might even be an act of love to let someone throw herself out of the window, at a certain point! The alternative is to lock her in a pigpen, like Vincenzo Muccioli did with one of the drug addicts he was treating, letting him die "for his own good."[8] There is a violence at the origin of history, and it's called authoritarianism, the failure to respect the other as myself, to love him. All this is the origin of evil.

I don't now know whether original sin exists, but what I believe we all ought to do is reduce violence rather than acknowledge it. Here is where Girard the anthropologist prevails over Girard the political Christian, in the sense that, according to him, when this cognizance of the anthropological truth becomes common knowledge, like that of science, then we will inhabit a more just, less violent world. Here my own deeply critical stance vis-à-vis science emerges clearly because for me science is linked to technology, which is no more or less than the imposition of a rational order on the world (and on this aspect, from what Girard says, I think he might agree with me). Hence on this point I continue to dissent. I haven't converted, nor, I fear, have I managed to convert Girard.

GIRARD: Personally, I agree with Vattimo when he says that Christianity is a revelation of love, but I don't exclude that it is also a revelation of *truth*. Because in Christianity truth and love coincide and are one and the same. I think we ought to take very seriously this concept: the concept of love, which in Christianity is the rehabilitation of the unjustly accused victim, which is truth itself, which is the anthropological truth and the Christian truth. And I think that this anthropological truth can impart to Christianity the anthropology it deserves. Because traditionally, Christian theology, which is essentially correct, has been based on the "wrong" anthropology: on Greek anthropology, which is a pagan anthropology, which doesn't discern mankind's responsibility as violent beings. I, on the other hand, believe that it is finally time to give Christian theology the anthropology it deserves to have.

2 | FAITH AND RELATIVISM
Gianni Vattimo and René Girard

PIERPAOLO ANTONELLO: One of the major topics of debate in recent years in Italy has been the disconnect between faith and relativism or, to put it another way, between universalism, whether anthropological or moral, on the one hand, and multicultural relativism, on the other. Obviously, you both start from essentially different positions in philosophical terms, but I would like to probe a bit to see what kind of reconciliation (if any) might be possible between these two positions.

GIANNI VATTIMO: Let me state my convictions with respect to relativism: from René Girard I took the idea that God can only be a relativist—not the easiest view to defend, I know—because the desacralizing thrust of Christianity (the extreme point of which is the Pauline *kénosis*, in other words the incarnation and humiliation) seems to me fundamentally to point toward the idea that God is not the content of a true proposition but is actually *someone* incarnated in Jesus Christ, and Jesus Christ is an exemplar of charity. I also take heart from the fact that the new pope's first encyclical bears the title *Deus caritas est*, and not *Deus veritas est*, which would have raised my hackles somewhat. I have to admit that my enthusiasm dwindled when I read the full text; still, this fact is very important. I think of God as relativist because he is the only entity who really could be, given that he gazes down on the various cultures of humanity from on high. God is not the content of a proposition; he is a person who walked among us and left us an example of charity. Apart from anything else, that gives the lie to the slogan that is always adduced to justify the burning of heretics or books: "Amicus Plato sed magis amica veritas" [Plato a friend, but truth a greater one]. I would be inclined to attribute to René Girard the slogan "Amica veritas sed magis amicus Plato" [truth a friend, but Plato a greater one], and I certainly wouldn't want to do away with poor Plato in the name of truth, although, come to that, you could argue that he deserved it . . .

RENÉ GIRARD: I don't see the proposition "Amica veritas sed magis amicus Plato" as differing very much from its converse. For me they are the same thing. I will tell you the reason I cannot be a relativist. I view the relativism of our day as an outcome of the failure of modern anthropology, of the attempt to resolve problems arising out of the diversity of human cultures. The mimetic theory is an effort to demonstrate that cultural differences, no matter how significant they may be at one level, are insignificant at another. There exist thousands of ways to codify and regulate social coexistence, like the laws concerning marriage, for example. But all these approaches have a single goal, that of preventing conflict and so transforming individuals who might experience reciprocal hatred into people capable of mutual amity. Analysis of these cultures makes it possible to identify thousands of buffers that are interposed between potential rivals—buffers that vary, because the problems to be dealt with are various, but that always have the same purpose. I have never ceased to believe that behind relativism there exists a unity of cognizance, which could only exist if this premise is accepted. The principal aim of my work has been to demonstrate that this is true in the most controversial area of all, by which I mean modern anthropology. Anthropology has failed because it was unable to account for the different human cultures as a unitary phenomenon, and that is why today we find ourselves bogged down in relativism. I have absolutely no wish to impose my own point of view, but it is difficult for me to simply forget the absolute aspects. And in my view Christianity offers a solution to these problems precisely because it demonstrates that the buffers, the limits that individuals reciprocally impose on themselves, serve to avoid a certain type of conflict. If it were understood that Jesus is the universal victim who came for the purpose of overcoming these conflicts, the problem would be resolved.

VATTIMO: I am quite convinced that on these topics Girard, as an anthropologist, has it right: I do not think that all anthropologies are equally true or equally false either, and Girard's defense of his own anthropology seems to be unassailable because, in a certain sense, it constitutes a "scientific truth." It's the same as in physics: not all hypotheses in physics can be considered equal. On the other hand, I am not entirely convinced that modernity, or contemporary relativism, at any rate, is dependent on the failure of anthropology. Has any of us ever met a *relativist*? An interview that Paul Ricoeur gave to *Le Monde* not long before his death comes to mind. He was asked if he was a relativist, and he replied: "I don't know. If you ask me what I believe, my answer is that on the basis of my experience, of the books I have read, of my vocation in this epoch, here I stand." He was echoing Luther's famous words, "Hier bin Ich." I myself have never known a relativist, just as I have never known anyone who said, "All theories, including mine, have equal value." So my suspicion is that today much of the outcry against relativism— I don't mean from Girard—is an outcry against liberalism in society: only a liberal society can be relativist because it has to allow different currents of opinion. If I wished to mend my own fault of relativism, as the pope demands, what would I have to do? What is it the pope wants? For me to think that he alone is right? I don't really see relativism as a mistaken theory because it isn't a theory. If anything, it is a doctrine of society, but in society, for reasons of charity, we have to allow different points of view, and in general I stake out this position: let's not say that we will reach agreement once we have found the truth. Let's say we have found the truth when we have reached agreement.

It is still possible to speak of truth, you understand, but only because we have realized *caritas* through agreement. *Caritas* with respect to opinion, with respect to choices about values, will become the truth when it is shared. Richard Rorty, for example, who is certainly not a Girardian thinker (or maybe he is without knowing it), proposes substituting the term "solidarity" for the term "truth," and I come right out and propose to make "charity" the substitute because all the rest is just opinion. Or else, in the case of anthropological truth, there certainly exist criteria within individual domains, as in the various languages of Wittgenstein, valid for establishing whether something works or not, but this merely signifies a truth determined on the basis of paradigms that are themselves historical. All I mean to say is that the problem of relativism seems to me more social than individual in kind.

When I hear the adversaries of relativism talking, I ask myself what I ought to do: stop being liberal? Relativism arises only in society, in the group, in the culture. Individuals may change opinions, and in this sense I too am a relativist, because if someone convinces me tomorrow that I have got it wrong, I am ready to alter my views. But above all, I think that my statement that

God can only be a relativist is highly consequential because the salvation of souls simply cannot depend on the content of certain propositions: you can be saved even if you are unacquainted with the doctrine of the Trinity.

GIRARD: I agree with Vattimo when he speaks about the practical necessity to identify oneself as relativist in a modern society. It is very interesting, I think, because my aim, the contribution I believe I make with my work, lies in showing that in its relation to the other religions, Christianity is infinitely more complex and comprehensive (in the sense that it is able to take in, to incorporate) than it may appear. The archaic religions existed for 50,000 years, each differing from the next, but all of them, in a certain sense, pre-Christian forms, forms that fell short of Christianity precisely because they believed in the guilt of the victim and did not recognize his or her innocence. Christianity reveals the error, affirms that these victims were innocent, just as Jesus is innocent. This is absolutely fundamental, and is interpretable, I think, Vattimo-style . . .

VATTIMO: [laughing] A "Vattimary" [*vattimaria*] religion instead of a "victimary" [*vittimaria*] one . . .

GIRARD: Far from being combative and menacing, Christianity unveils the conflict on which the religions are founded, and the injustice suffered by the victims who were condemned but who were all fundamentally innocent, like Christ. Through his deed Jesus unveils the unspoken innocence, the misunderstanding, hidden beneath the blood of history.

VATTIMO: I, too, define myself as Christian because I believe that Christianity is more "true" than all the other religions precisely on account of the fact that there is a sense in which *it is not a religion*. No doubt there does exist a dogmatic content, but, for example, when we recite the *Credo*, we use a number of purely metaphorical, allegorical expressions: Jesus is seated at the right hand of the Father. Really! What about the left-hand side? Politically, it's a bit biased! And then God is a male, a father, but never a mother: that gets the blood of American feminists boiling. A great many things in the *Credo* can't be taken literally. I personally am convinced that I do believe inasmuch as I strive to respect charity (something at which I don't always succeed), not inasmuch as I affirm that only men can be priests and not women—or take sides in any of the other squabbles that make the life of the churches so effervescent. When I repeat my favorite motto, "Thank God I'm an atheist," what I mean is that luckily Jesus Christ has set me free from belief in idols, in divinities, in natural laws, and so on, and so in this sense I define myself as an atheist. But an atheist only with respect to the God of the philosophers, obviously, meaning God as "pure act," omniscience, and so on. I always feel highly faithful to Girard, and I can even keep that faith when he is absent.

GIRARD: I'm pretty sure I agree. In this sense Christianity is the most radical critique of the ancient religions, especially the archaic ones, that you can find. In the archaic religions, the role of the victim was misunderstood: the victim became a divinity through guiltiness, a miraculous being precisely by virtue of his guilt. From a "technical" point of view, Christianity is the interpretive key for understanding mythology. Of the claims I advance, the one that seems to provoke the most outrage among anthropologists is this: if you want to understand mythology, if you want to solve the riddle of myth, turn to Christianity. Once you grasp the fact that Oedipus is accused of parricide and incest (not just by Freud, by the Greeks) whereas in reality he is innocent, and that Jesus, innocent as well, is accused of the same crimes in certain folk beliefs, then it becomes clear that, through Christianity, myth can be read in a completely different manner.

ANTONELLO: On that basis, I would like to cite something Gianni Vattimo said to the effect that "the very idea of the pluralism of cultures exists, and has developed, within a specific culture, that of the West." Girard expresses the same concept when he states that Christianity has an enhanced capacity for understanding the victim mechanisms that are the foundation of cultural construction. So I would like to ask: How is it possible to begin an interconfessional dialogue from this presupposition not of superiority but of an enhanced capacity on the part of Christianity and the West?

VATTIMO: I think that the position sketched by Antonello can only be held acceptably if we come to the dialogue unburdened by strong theoretical content, because otherwise quarrels about the nature of God soon flare up. There is a phrase in the New Testament that says, "Everything that was written long ago in the scriptures was meant to teach us something" (Romans 15:4), which amounts to saying: the Bible is neither a handbook of cosmology nor a handbook of anthropology nor even a handbook of theology because the things recounted about God in the Bible are very often mythical. I would have difficulty from the theoretical standpoint in reconciling the God who commands the Hebrews to exterminate the babies of Babylon with the God of Jesus Christ. I believe that what's good about Christianity is that it has drained pretty much all force from the word "true." Dietrich Bonhoeffer said "Einen Gott, den 'es gibt,' gibt es nicht," "There is no God who 'is there.'"[1] In other words, God is not an object, nor can his existence be an article of faith. What does it mean to say that God exists? Where? Here, or in heaven, or hiding under the table, or only in church? Jesus says that when two or three people come together in his name, he is with them. But did he mean that he is there *also*, or that he is *only* there? There is no telling where God might be. We can gather anywhere, but that doesn't mean that God resides in certain privileged places like sanctuaries, churches, temples. The point of all this is that the ecumenical mission of Christianity seems to me strictly dependent on its stripping itself of its claim to lay down metaphysical declarations, to define human nature or what God is like or how human societies are and so on. As I've said already, I greatly respect the tradition of the saints, but with that I intend to express respect for the tradition, not for nature or objective truth.

GIRARD: There is a domain of human conduct that Vattimo has failed to mention: morality. I would like to ask him this: Does what he says imply or not imply, include or not include, the Ten Commandments and Leviticus. That is, do not kill, do not commit adultery, do not desire the wife of another or the goods of another. Don't the Ten Commandments actually entail a notion of morality? Are they not implicit in the notion of charity? Or are they only the expression of a puritan mentality, a deleterious morality? I would like to know what he thinks about the Ten Commandments.

VATTIMO: Let me make a brief digression before getting to the heart of the question. Just recently I took part in a debate on the story of David and Jonathan. Did these two men love one other in homoerotic terms, or were they just good friends? So I looked up the passage in Scripture where it says that if you are a man you must not lie with another man as you would with a woman (Leviticus 20:13). But this commandment occurs in the midst of a whole series of other things: for example, "You must not eat things that creep on the ground," or, "You must not wear red garments." The point is, it is mixed in with a lot of other Judeo-biblical prescriptions that no one heeds any more. Like when someone brushes against a pig and then has to go and wash himself in the purificatory pool. The Ten Commandments, of course, have come down to us with much greater authority and are widely heeded, so much so that many people think of them as natural law. Then again, in the Christian tradition the commandment not to kill very often comes with conditions attached: if you kill a man on this side of the river, as Pascal said, you are an assassin, if you kill him on that side of the river (the river being the border of your country), you are a hero and when you come home they give you a medal. And there were the Crusades and the Inquisition. I do not believe in the absoluteness of the principle of not killing. Faced with a person who is suffering greatly and who asks me to assist him with euthanasia, I will try to encourage him, I'll read him uplifting books, I'll show him beautiful films, but if despite all that he really wants to die, the one thing I must not violate is his liberty, by which I mean his soul, not his physical life. Tumors are full of physical life too, they replicate themselves furiously. . . . As I've said more than once: the guideline is the principle of charity plus the traffic rules. I respect the traffic rules not because a natural law dictates that I should but simply because I don't want to injure someone or get injured myself. It is always the imperative of charity that forbids me to do something. And so, to the best of my ability anyway, I respect the Ten Commandments, too; I recognize an important element of reason in them. For example: Can I love Plato more than I love truth? Or, regarding the prohibition on killing: If a woman who has been raped during the interethnic conflict in Bosnia decides to have an abortion, what should I do? Help her or force her to give birth? If she requests help in a case like that, it's the charitable imperative that compels me to agree. As for the sixth commandment, the prohibition on adultery, don't get me started on that. It concerns love and charity—which the pope, naturally, distinguishes with great severity, as though *agape* and *eros* were two entirely different things. If I have to break off an amorous relationship, a homosexual one, let's say, because I have converted to Christianity, do I then have to abandon my partner? Like when God slaughters Job's family and livestock to put him to the test?

GIRARD: One of the most important passages in the Bible, I think, is the one in which God gives the Ten Commandments to Moses, because we have to consider what type of world it was into which they were introduced, a world with thousands of complicated laws. The simplicity and power of the Ten Commandments make them the most mystical document in the entire Old Testament. Vattimo is minimizing this potency a bit, I would say. He would have us believe that Christianity is the simplest and easiest of religions and that if we let ourselves go, abandon all scruples, there is a good chance that we will all wind up being able to do just as we please, living together happily. I am not sure it's true; I doubt it would be that easy, and the Ten Commandments clearly back me up. It seems to me that in presenting us with a sort of hedonistic Christianity, Vattimo is making life a little too simple for everybody. I don't think it is true that if all of us were to succeed in amusing ourselves in the right way and enjoying life, there wouldn't be any more problems. My feeling is that in life there will always be situations that will lead to conflict and that many of these are unavoidable.

VATTIMO: In debates I always tend to exaggerate. . . . Naturally I have the greatest respect for the Ten Commandments. Nonetheless, in regard to what Girard has said, it is precisely the idea of prohibition that strikes me most forcefully. When Jesus speaks of the *parousia*, the glorious return of Christ at the end of time, he doesn't explain how it will come about, but he does invite us not to believe in a list of things. I am most attracted to dialectical theology. Christianity teaches me that human laws hold good only up to a point. The reasonableness of the Ten Commandments is such that even if there were a dyed-in-the-wool secularist here, he would say that they suit him just fine. I truly believe that it is impossible to take seriously the ensemble of prohibitions that have been laid down. All in all I tend to think that Marcuse wasn't wrong and that what he proposed could not be realized only because society was and is repressive, authoritarian, proprietary. Wasn't Jesus on my side, on Marcuse's? Why not make it our project to bring about a world in which the original communism of the Christian communities is realized? In his encyclical the pope says that it has vanished, as though that were a fact of nature. Holding their possessions in common was precisely the way that the first Christians practiced charity. In the encyclical *Deus caritas est*, the pope acknowledges the existence of this aspect but then takes for granted, as a matter of fact, that it is gone for good. It used to be taken for granted that Christians ought to go on crusades and kill their enemies, too. We can't accept that all these utopian contents (utopian in the sense that they are now outmoded), like original Christian communism or harmony in society, have to fail perforce. Let's not surrender completely to anthropology (and for that matter, I've never studied any anthropology except Girard's, which I greatly esteem) and believe, as the pope does, that the communism of the early church could never have lasted, human nature being what it is. Didn't it turn out that way because the church compromised too much with worldly power? Much of the prestige of the Ten Commandments depends on the type of society in which they are embedded. The commandment not to desire another man's wife keeps men from fighting to the death with knives over women. But today we have divorce: we have institutionalized one more freedom that doesn't fit in with the Ten Commandments. The Ten Commandments were valid at that time, in that society.

A MEMBER OF THE PUBLIC: I would like to put a question to Girard in relation to a theme that is central to Gianni Vattimo's thinking (and not just his): philosophical nihilism. Could he discuss his position with respect to contemporary nihilism, especially from an ethical-moral perspective?

GIRARD: With respect to moral nihilism, I would state the following. People think that most of the conflicts today are caused by absolute values, absolute opinions about this or that, what are called "ideologies" or "grand narratives"; they think that absolute opinions generate violence because they generate opposition. There is something aggressive about that, and I think it is a mistaken way of viewing violence in our world, and violence in general. Most anthropologists and sociologists still define violence as aggression, but human violence is not aggressive. The word "aggression" is itself very aggressive because if we define violence as aggression, it's a characteristic that nobody would acknowledge in himself. We define violence as something that pertains to others; it's they who are aggressive, or aggressors. But it isn't true. There is no form of violence in which the actors overtly identify as violent aggressors. Man is essentially competitive and inclined to rivalry. He wants to outdo his neighbor, and so he competes with him. Human intelligence, the spirit of initiative, is basically competitive. So it can have great value, as we well know. But it becomes violence when the degree of

59

GIANNI VATTIMO *and* RENÉ GIRARD

competition rises to the point of spilling over into destructive rivalry. This is true for animals as well. When a male animal sees another male seeking to possess a female, it desires that female too. It doesn't see itself as an aggressor but as a rival for the conquest of that female. It feels it has the same rights as the others. This is a process that we are able in most cases to channel positively (it sums up economics in a nutshell), but it can also spill over into violence. Hence the situation is a lot more ambivalent and complex than it seems because *all of us* are caught up in these forms of reciprocal rivalry, the effects of which can simultaneously be positive and negative. Moreover, when we analyze a violent situation, we always define it as aggression coming from the other party, and of course the other party does likewise. Nine times out of ten it's not aggressiveness that underlies violence but competition, in which both parties take part: both individuals are equally right and wrong; they both behave in equal, symmetrical fashion. The situation is inextricable and cannot be resolved through "legal" means. That is why archaic societies tried to channel competition in a very precise direction, constraining individuals to desire one thing rather than another, to go in one direction rather than another. This may limit individual freedom of enterprise—and a dynamic civilization may not even be possible within certain boundaries—but very often societies are forced to establish them to keep competition from spilling over into destructive violence. As I said, this problem is social in character, and it cannot easily be fixed with laws, which is why charity, as Vattimo and I have said, is so important. But these are infinitely complex problems, to which no verbal or ideological solution exists, no solution that language can bring about. Human relations are simply too complex, and we tend to avoid facing this fact because each of us is fighting for his or her own personal position. The mimetic theory addresses all this directly.

Philosophical nihilism, I would hazard, arises from the fact that we come to realize that our language does not coincide with human reality, which resists translation into words. So the nihilist surrenders the attempt to explain it, asserting that the problem is insoluble. That's not my view. I see the current form of nihilism as the failure of what we call the Enlightenment, the rational vision of the universe elaborated by the eighteenth century. In this rational vision, human relations become too complex to analyze (and so in compensation we have the unsurpassed perspicacity of the modern novel). In my view, instead of giving up and drifting into some form of nihilism, asserting like some philosophers that there exists no certain truth, we must return to anthropology and psychology and study human relations better than they have been studied to date. We need a much more subtle analysis of human relations, and I believe the mimetic theory can supply the tools of observation, and a level of analysis at which human conflict may become more intelligible—not any easier to resolve, of course, but comprehensible. I hold that it is possible through the mimetic theory to understand the complex dynamic of social and human relations, and this can steer us away from the type of nihilism, the type of cognitive renunciation, we have today.

VATTIMO: My own nihilism does not come down to the thesis that there exist no truths, as Girard well knows, so I feel challenged only in part. The dissolution of absolutes, and hence of the conviction that human nature can be known, seems to me a positive effect of Christianity. At bottom, the very notion of creation stands absolutely opposed to a vision of objectivity; God the creator has nothing of the rigorous rationality of Aristotle's pure Act, which would never have been able to "decide" at a given moment to create a world. In sum, the only thing I really can't go along with in Girard is his faith in the salvific power of truth, whether it be revealed or discovered by science.

A MEMBER OF THE PUBLIC: Professor Girard, it results clearly from your work that Jesus is the one who proclaimed, and bore witness to, the innocence of the victim, and in this way unmasked the victim mechanism present in mythology and the pre-Christian religions. Yet Jesus transmits another message to us as well, at least in the tradition: he is also the judge, the one who declares that the persecutors of today will be the persecuted ones tomorrow. The victim mechanism isn't put to an end once and for all because it seems almost as if the executioners of today will become the victims of tomorrow in the proclamation of eternal damnation as the destiny awaiting all those who do not convert. In the course of history different interpretations have been advanced; one thinks of Origen. But the Catholic Church, and the Protestant churches too, insist on clinging to eternal damnation. I would like to ask you for some interpretive guidance.

GIRARD: The theological and ecclesiastical interpretations of Christianity do indeed transform Jesus into a judge, which is more or less the exact opposite of what he is. Today there is a fervent reaction against the ecclesiastical vision of the world and against the punitive and drastic aspects of Christianity. These form part of a great drama, a spectacle, and perhaps it ought to be staged some other way. But if we were to get rid of all the sanctions and all these, so to speak, "theatrical" and dramatic aspects, we would be eliminating an extremely important part of our lives. Consider the novel, for example: in novels our existence is seen more as comedy than as tragedy, but there is something at stake in every event. The great power of the idea of heaven and hell is precisely that it supplies motivation for our lives, transforms them into a dramatic representation. Without these aspects, religion would lose the greater part of its own force. Frequently in literature, in the catechism, or in theology, we encounter this "punitive" portrayal of heaven and hell, which may be simplistic, but which, from a different point of view, endows Christianity with something it cannot do without, on penalty of losing all its special force. Our nature as aesthetic creatures is very important. We are beings both aesthetic and ethical at the same time. If we were to strip Christianity of all these tragic aspects, all the ingenuous expression of faith that lies in the contrast among heaven, hell, and purgatory, what would become of Dante, one of the greatest writers who ever lived, who bases his *Divine Comedy* on exactly that division? What would become of Italian literature? Extremely simple and ingenuous it may be, but without the contrast of paradise, inferno, and purgatory, the *Divine Comedy* would lose all its power. Do you Italians have any comment on that?

ANTONELLO: Indeed the great power of Dante, at once expressive and theological-moral, is grounded in his extraordinary realism, his adherence to a strong human reality, and that is one of the most distinctive characteristics of the Christian vision of the world, as Erich Auerbach suggested in *Mimesis*. The *Divine Comedy* describes a world beyond this world, but with such rootedness in the historical, personal, and material reality of individuals that it can still speak to modern man, who continues to construct his own proper hells on earth and to attempt difficult purgatories. Umberto Eco has emphasized that Dante's *Inferno* continues to say something to us precisely because, unlike medieval man, we have lost the strength to contemplate paradise—any paradise whatsoever—as well as the habit of doing so.

3 | HERMENEUTICS, AUTHORITY, TRADITION

Gianni Vattimo and René Girard

ROBERT HARRISON:[1] I would like to ask René Girard to comment on the particular reading that Gianni Vattimo has given to his work by reinterpreting it in a Heideggerian key.

RENÉ GIRARD: I may not be the person best qualified to supply a response to Gianni Vattimo in strictly philosophical terms, but I must say nevertheless that I find myself in agreement with the bulk of what he has to say, especially when it comes to his claim about the relation between Heidegger and the Judeo-Christian scriptures. There have been numerous attempts, especially in France, to study the relation between Heidegger and the problem of God, but I have the impression that they have all glanced off the most important questions. For my part I believe that the closest links are to be found in the hermeneutic perspective, the end of metaphysics, and, especially, "productive" interpretation. A propos of this, I take the view that the Old Testament should be the point of departure, because it seems to me that the question of interpretation is already central in that very text. The Old Testament is already available to be read as an interpretive system. In Genesis, for example, the story of Joseph can be read as *an interpretation of myth*. Joseph is the mythical figure of the hero who is the victim of his own brothers, of the group he himself belongs to, and like many mythical figures (think of Oedipus), he is accused of having committed a sexual crime. Hence he is expelled, first from his own family and then from his adoptive country, as the person whose crime provoked the terrible plague that afflicts his people. The question posed by mythical texts and the Bible text is the same: "Is he guilty?" Myth always answers in the affirmative. Oedipus is guilty and his relatives and friends have the right to drive him out. But in the Old Testament story, the answer given is the opposite: Joseph is innocent, and his brothers, who are jealous, drive him out unjustly and hound him in mimetic fashion. So right from the start the Bible presents itself as an interpretation of mythology, and as a deconstruction of it.

In this sense I can say that I agree with Vattimo, even though my own trajectory and method of reasoning are different, primarily because I have to define myself as a "bad" Heideggerian, despite the fact that I have read Heidegger with some care. I only took an interest in some parts of Heidegger, and since I have always focused more on anthropology than philosophy, I have a more restricted vocabulary than does Vattimo, who certainly has a better title to the status of "creative Heideggerian" than I do. He is one of the few philosophers around who makes use of Heidegger in an original manner, reinterpreting him in new directions. And the idea that Christ is living interpretation seems highly valid to me. There is something missing in Vattimo's discourse, though: the fact that, at the culminating moment of the story of Jesus, we have his Passion, in other words, the fact that he dies, and dies a violent death at that. From my perspective, the difference between the stories in the Old Testament, like the story of Joseph, and the gospel, is that in the gospel not only do we find the deconstruction of pagan, archaic myth, but this deconstruction is initiated by a death, which is like all the other mythical deaths except that the reader no longer believes in the guilt of the victim. The gospel shows us the whole panorama of mythology in a nutshell, in other words, its mimetic genesis, through the behavior of the crowd, a crowd that in the Bible never stands for reason but is always on the side of the violent persecutors.

I say this in order to support what Vattimo asserts, which is something very hard to state today, at a historical moment when the majority of the institutions, the intellectual groupings, even churches that are directly connected to the Judeo-Christian tradition—and this is something really ironic—are striving with all their might to pretend that they aren't that at all, or to uncouple themselves from Christianity, or to consider it as something pestilential. In our politically correct world, we consider the Judeo-Christian tradition as the only one that bears a stain, while all the others are exempt from any possible form of criticism. The Christian religion cannot even be mentioned in certain settings, or it can only be discussed in order to keep it under control, keep it in check, on the pretext that there is nothing positive in it, indeed, on the grounds that it bears prime and sole responsibility for the horrors of the modern world. And it seems to me that there is a remarkable irony in the fact that the people who completely abandoned this tradition are now beginning to take a fresh interest in these problems—especially the most influential sector of the avant-garde, to which Vattimo undoubtedly belongs. That is, they are taking a new interest in the most important aspects of the hermeneutic tradition from which we all come, saying things that are obvious from where I stand but that are novel in the context of Heideggerian exegesis.

Naturally I have a few problems with some aspects of Vattimo's position, for example, with respect to the problem of *authority*. He works from within the deconstructive tradition, to which

I, too, belong in a certain sense, but I believe he forgets or neglects the extent to which the problem of the crowd is central within the framework of Judeo-Christian interpretation. I think that the limits to Vattimo's analysis originate in the enormous error committed by Nietzsche, whom I regard as the greatest theologian of modern times (something many people don't know). Nietzsche, in the last months of his life, on the brink of madness, says something extremely important, something that Heidegger deliberately ignored because Heidegger—who was a formidable engine of self-promotion right from the start of his career—had grasped that it was necessary to get rid of the religious problematic in Nietzsche, and he did so by simply declaring that Nietzsche had a problem of personal rivalry with the monotheistic traditions. His advice was to pay no attention to whatever Nietzsche had to say about the matter: the only relevant Nietzsche was the Greek, Dionysiac Nietzsche. On the contrary, the most important thing Nietzsche ever said about religion (and, I would hazard, the most important thing said in theology since the time of Saint Paul) is that in myth the victim is always expelled and justly killed (and in this sense, I, too, could claim to be a bit of a Nietzschean), whereas the community bears no blame. Sacrifice is something necessary and therefore positive because a community, a society, that cannot kill, that cannot victimize, no matter if the victims are innocent, is condemned to extinction; it is condemned to exactly the kind of weakness we have today, a weakness inherited from Christianity. With this I don't intend to make Nietzsche into a precursor of Nazism, but he was clearly a man who found it unbearable to live in a world that was already politically correct *avant la lettre*.

So where does Nietzsche's interpretation go awry? He asserts that the ferocity of the Dionysiac is a characteristic that society ought to preserve and that Christianity is destroying the world because it is too "tender," because it opposes sacrifice and any form of victimization—and here is where I see him as more profound than any modern theologian because he *chooses* to take the part of violence! And Heidegger defuses this whole discourse, advising against reading this part of Nietzsche and remaking him into a philosopher who can be read at once as politically correct and as someone who asserts that "there are no facts, only interpretations." But the real Nietzsche is much more ambivalent, and Vattimo, I believe, knows it.

In the end my objection to Vattimo would be this: he talks about a history of interpretation that develops within a community, among groups of people who love one another and have no need for forms of "authority" to regulate their internal relations. But what I ask myself is: How do we control the ever-present tendency of the crowd to veer off into some excess? How can we tell whether this love arising in its midst is true love and not just the reciprocal indifference of the "politically correct"? We preach our opposition to any form of persecution, but we may still be trapped in a victim logic, continuing to persecute those who tarnished themselves with persecution in the past. In a politically correct culture, with individuals cooped up in one identity or another, that is what typically happens. Are we quite sure that we are building a world capable of resisting these mechanisms, with which the history of humanity is studded and which we continue to observe all around us?

In a certain way, the fact that the Bible uses mythical language instead of the positivistic language of the natural sciences signifies precisely—in the case of the Bible and only in the case of the Bible—that its knowledge is not metaphysical. I can't prove this explicitly, but I think that in Vattimo's conclusions there arises the problem of how this new interpretation emerges without turning into the destructive form of nihilism, because the curious thing is that the only individuals who are keeping alive the traditions to which Vattimo refers are the very same ones who are upholding the church's structure of authority. Leaving the Catholic Church aside, we could ponder what has happened to the Protestant world, for example, with its fragmentation into thousands of confessions and congregations, or what has happened to Orthdoxy, the Russian and Byzantine church, which, however decadent it may appear in some respects, has kept alive a tradition in a way very different and robust from the way that prevails in the West.

The problem is that our discussion so far hasn't ranged beyond a Heideggerian horizon; we haven't escaped a purely linguistic problematic, whereas we ought to be looking at things historically and anthropologically. When I refer to authority, I am not referring to dictatorial power or political authority; I am talking about the authority, or the authoritativeness, of *ritual*. About religion, in other words, and thought as action, as a sort of routine, of repeated action, because ritual is basically repetition. Ritual is a collective action meant to prevent the crowd from losing control. We don't live in a perfect world, of course. Historically it's the case that Christianity has been seeking to eliminate ritual, but notwithstanding this—or perhaps I should say this comes about because—primitive Christianity was aware that it always needed to preserve a certain "quantity" of ritual, which is unavoidable. The bare bones of the ecclesiastical structure, and the apparatus of ritual, are both aimed instrumentally at preventing human groups from self-igniting into lynch mobs. So whenever I speak of authority, I am always referring to ritual.

GIANNI VATTIMO: I will try to respond to the objections of Girard, and will address what he asserts to be the limits of secularization and the criteria of this secularization. Is it possible to formulate criteria for love within a community, distinct from the mimetically violent crowd? I believe that there is a problem of interpretation about just what the term *charity* means within the Christian tradition. Girard clearly has strong interpretive reasons to express suspicion about the crowd, which can coalesce mimetically against anyone, anytime, but I balk at accepting reasons of an excessively humanistic kind for being against the crowd. There is a page from Ernst Bloch's book *Spirit of Utopia* that always springs to mind, mine anyway, where he says that for him Christ can be compared to a clown more than he can to a tragic hero.[2] And I don't believe he meant it all that disrespectfully because in Christianity there is a deconstruction of sorts, a dissolving of the power claims of the forces of evil: Jesus doesn't combat Satan through struggle but with irony: "Death, where is your victory?" [1 Cor 15:55]. Death gains victory when we take it too seriously. Furthermore, only with the decline of subjectivity, and that includes the utopian subjectivity of the struggling tragic hero, can there arise a new relation of friendship and familiarity between man and the world.

So I tend to think that I ought to have a more open attitude toward the crowd, although I obviously disapprove on the occasions when it veers off into criminality and violence. In post-metaphysical thought, truth can only be conceived in terms of "participation." But this fact has a hard time gaining acceptance. Take Habermas's theory of communicative action; I disagree with Habermas about many things, but on this point I do share his views: truth and rationality can only be conceived in terms of the communicability of questions, persuasiveness, and so on. That this entails risk is something of which I am well aware. We haven't really got to a position very far in advance of other historical phases or other "civilizations," and we do have to make a distinction between *caritas* and an overindulgent attitude toward the mimetic passions of the crowd. It is also true that for the romantic writers of the late eighteenth and early nineteenth centuries—Schelling, Hölderlin, Novalis—church and state were two separate communities, and the true community was the church, understood as the *authentic* community and not as the hierarchical church or the ecclesiastical apparatus. The church was the community of *caritas*, while the state was the secular, worldly community, and there was inevitably a battle between the *civitas dei* (the city of God) and the *civitas diaboli* (the city of the devil). I don't believe I have a philosophical solution to all this, but since I am one of the exponents of what has come to be known as "weak thought," which is precisely a theory of weakness and weakening, I do believe steadfastly in my own attempt to link the criteria for community to the criteria for the dissolution of the force of Being. If community is the criterion I use to impose some limits on the process of secularization, it is because I believe in weakening the power structures of Being. The criterion of weakening is also what guides me in my assessment of what counts as a just community. Let me give a simple example. When Khomeini took over in Iran, many of my Foucaldian friends, and even Foucault himself, saw this as an important event of liberation because it was autochthonous, brought about by a real community.

But what criterion do I apply in order to assess that community? It's the criterion that comes from the reasons I accept community, meaning the reduction of violence and the dissolution of the power structures of Being. I don't take community itself as the overriding criterion. Community becomes a criterion at the moment at which I realize that the history of Being is destined to dwindle, to shrink in force and importance and to deconstruct violence. Obviously we are not talking about straightforward processes, but I believe that it is possible to judge what is acceptable and what isn't when it comes to the crowd, and I believe that several readings of the Old Testament put forward by Girard are stimulating and important for the type of analysis and the philosophical stance that I defend.

STUDENT: I wanted to put a further question to Vattimo concerning a problem central to understanding the mechanisms of persecution in Girard: the problem of the crowd, to which we all belong, and the role of the individual in that setting. I wonder whether the "productivity" of interpretation, its possibility and its diffusion, might not also be linked to the dimension of the crowd, with its plurality and complexity, and consequently linked to the risk of violence that can always erupt from it. The productivity of interpretation and the risk of crowd violence would, so to speak, go hand in hand.

VATTIMO: In one sense I agree, because the idea of the dissolution of an objective truth also produces the liberation of the will to power. It is not an accident that in *The Will to Power*, Nietzsche spoke of the multiplicity of interpretation. The question is always the same: you said correctly that we ourselves are the crowd, but if someone asks me "how can I set limits on the crowd?" I feel absolutely no inclination to answer him, because I myself am the crowd! We are all, individually, inside the crowd, and that includes the handful of people listening to us right now. So far be it from me or anyone else to set limits on myself or others.

What I think when it comes to the crowd is that Nietzsche had his reasons for theorizing the *Übermensch* (usually translated "superman" but I prefer *oltreuomo*, literally "beyond-man").[3] In this situation of multiplying interpretations, man can only survive by going farther and becoming a new type, capable of devising and proposing ever new interpretations. This is connected to what Richard Rorty has to say about "redescription" and originality. His stance is a touch aestheticizing, no doubt, but in the last analysis it gets to the core of the problem because it arrives at the realization that there no longer exists an interpretation structurally strong and authoritarian. One has to become an interpreter, not just someone who is passively contemplating the truth, or what passes for such. Ritual practice could also be understood, once again, as a moment of maturation in the interpretation-constructing process, a way of rationalizing or reducing complexity. But here lies a problem: there is no return to metaphysical and structural modalities because it is impossible, all we can do is to push on ahead and create the beyond-man.

VAN HARVEY:[4] Even if it is possible to highlight an analogy between Heidegger and Girard regarding the deconstruction of metaphysics and the problem of violence, I can't imagine that Girard finds much to agree with in your postmodern notion of the deconstruction of subjectivity, because *agape* requires a subject, a person, in order to exist, and the victims are not just victims but subjects, real persons. In this sense I also have to dissent regarding the reduction of *agape* to victimization, because *agape* has to treat the persecutors as human beings, just like the victims. And I believe that the Heideggerian concept of *Ereignis*, which you use to define Being as "event" or "occurrence"[5] is substantially without content and entirely formalistic and that Heidegger did not really specify what it meant in relation to human events. We must regard it as a sort of mystical rupture within the temporal order. In the last years of his life he was much more attracted to Buddhism because he thought it was free of the personalistic emphasis found in Christianity. So I agree that Heidegger was and may still be profoundly implicated in questions of a theological kind, but I don't believe that *Ereignis* is a helpful concept in this domain.

VATTIMO: No disagreement about that, but what I have insisted on is that in order to develop the Heideggerian project, the deep reasons for his refusal of metaphysics have to be considered. It is true that *Ereignis* is a formal term, but the motivations that led Heidegger to consider Being as *Ereignis* rather than as object or ultimate foundation are motivations that lead in the direction of the reduction of violence. So if we are willing to read Heidegger in a way that goes a little farther than the letter of his text, I believe we must interpret his theory of the end of metaphysics toward a reduction of violence. Nor do I think the concept is an empty one because when I try to discuss modernity and postmodernity, I find it serviceable. When I talk about the dissolution of subjective consciousness as ultimate foundation, for example, I am also working against violence, precisely because those who exert forms of coercion and violence believe firmly that they are in the right, that they do so legitimately, and so on. Even slavery requires a subject on which it can be exercised, but if the subject is dissolved, nothing remains for it to inflict its violent dominion on. There is an effective way to reduce violence through reducing the force of our arguments about concepts like nature, being, and truth.

The notion of *Ereignis* even has its uses in thinking about what is taking place in the contemporary world, in the sense that in *Things Hidden*, apart from the anthropological vocabulary, there comes to the fore the idea of a completion of history, through which we find ourselves facing the choice between radical violence and the total acceptance of charity. I believe that this aspect, along with the question of the spirit and the church, can better be understood if we start from a Heideggerian position that elaborates a history of Being rather than presenting an apocalyptic vision. And I believe that this adds something to Girard's perspective that is missing in *Things Hidden*.

HARVEY: I wanted as well to ask Vattimo for some clarification regarding his concept of tradition, because I think it is too likely to slide into a sort of relativism. From my point of view, it is important for the community to bind itself together by deciding to submit to one "myth" and one only, that of Jesus Christ. That is the only basis upon which it is possible to establish what is violence and what isn't, and all the criteria for reducing it. Gianni Vattimo is no doubt aware of the work of Friedrich Gogarten, a German theologian whose views are close to his own on secularization as a positive event.[6] In this connection, I wish to state my own strong reservations about the relation between Christianity and secularization; these have to do with the absence of a transcendental dimension, which in secular culture disappears completely. It was precisely for this reason that many theologians like Karl Barth and Dietrich Bonhoeffer saw secularization as a desert, and I for my part see this as a bridge linking these Protestant theologians to Heidegger, who also expressed himself in ways that showed his unease about the desert of secularization. So I have difficulty in accepting this idea of a continuity between Christianity and secularization . . .

VATTIMO: On the problem of tradition and the unity of the "myth" or narration around which the unity of Christianity revolves, I would say first of all that myths, all of them, are things that can't easily be distinguished from their interpretation. For the rest, I concur with Girard that there is a difference between a myth like that of Oedipus and a "myth" like that of Christ. I, for my part, tend to place the emphasis on the notion of "transmission," on what Gadamer would call the *Wirkungsgeschichte*, the history of the effect something has had over time. Naturally it is continuity that represents unity in terms of *Wirkungsgeschichte*, the continuity of *discursus*, and *discursus* takes place within the church, but not just any one church—which brings us to the problem of ecumenism and the unity of Christianity. I would say that authority resides more in the continuity of this transmission than in the authority of any institution or any fixed reading of some sacred text. Maybe this is a reaction to my Catholic heritage because I was taught that the gospel came first, followed by Denzinger's *Enchiridion Symbolorum et Definitionum*, the standard collection of all the dogmatic creeds and definitions through the ages. So when I say that the church, understood as a community, ought to take the place of Denzinger, maybe all I am doing is reacting to my own experience!

As for the problem of transcendence, recently I read the latest version of the *Catechism of the Catholic Church* and I was pleased to observe that it no longer speaks of transcendence, because transcendence is a highly metaphysical notion that implies a distinction between a natural order and a supernatural order—and that way leads back to Aristotle. But if transcendence is called *charis*, meaning grace, the intervention of an illumination, then that is a perspective I could accept. In a certain sense there is an element of "transcendence" in history because if something new comes about in its course, that can be defined as a form of transcendence of history itself. Hence, from my point of view, the very notion of transcendence has to be reexamined.

Then, Professor Harvey mentioned the dialectical theology of the early twentieth century: I feel very remote from this tradition because from my perspective we are still dealing with a strongly metaphysical theology. To the extent that it is really focused on the world beyond, on transcendence, then this is something that cannot be accepted from a Heideggerian stance. So why did Heidegger get so deeply mixed up with people who come from this tradition? It's the same question that one can put with respect to his involvement with Nazism. I simply believe that he misinterpreted some of the implications of his own thought. I daresay that my interpretation of Heidegger arises out of the fact that, as I always say, I understand Heidegger better than he understood himself! I consider myself a "left" Heideggerian, not just for political reasons but also on account the parallel with Hegelianism, because what I try to do is to develop an interpretation of Heidegger that takes seriously the negative notion of Being, Being as a sort of apophatic theology,[7] not something with a factual existence out there in three-dimensional space. In this respect, I believe that the contribution Heidegger offers for our understanding of the perspectives more or less explicitly put forward by Girard in his works, and for extending them in a progressive sense, is absolutely essential.

4 | HEIDEGGER AND GIRARD
Kénosis and the End of Metaphysics
Gianni Vattimo

> Heidegger becomes crystal clear when we read him, not in a philosophical light but in the light, not really of anthropology, but of the "meta-anthropology" we have been sketching out. Meta-anthropology does not satisfy me but it refers to what happens when the scapegoat mechanism is at last detected, and the multiplicity of meanings attached to the sacred is understood, not as a form of thought that mixes everything up together (as with Lévy-Bruhl and Lévi-Strauss) but as the original matrix of human thought—the cauldron in which not only our cultural institutions but all our modes of thought were forged, through a process of successive differentiation.
>
> **GIRARD**, *THINGS HIDDEN SINCE THE FOUNDATION OF THE WORLD*

The short testimony I want to contribute to this colloquium about René Girard may very well start with this quotation from *Things Hidden*. My purpose is to show how the work of Girard has helped me to "complete" Heidegger, to clarify the meaning of his thought and eventually to reopen communication between (some part of) contemporary postmetaphysical philosophy and the Judeo-Christian tradition. This testimony is also meant as a thanks offering to Girard for all that I believe I have learned from him, although in doing so I may well have committed misunderstandings or distortions of his original intentions.

Girard, in the well known lines which conclude the second book of *Things Hidden*, insists upon the fact that Heidegger, although he did recognize a deep difference between the Greek *logos* of Heraclitus and the *logos* of the gospel of Saint John, remained completely within the victimary logic that dominates the main line of modern thought. In particular, Heidegger offers emblematic evidence of the "expulsion" the Judeo-Christian Scriptures have undergone in modernity. It is indeed striking that Heidegger, in retrieving the history of European ontotheology, completely ignores the explicitly theological aspects of this process: what he recounts is only the history of metaphysical ontology, without any allusion to the Bible. Nevertheless, says Girard, "Heidegger, like any true thinker, participates in spite of himself in the immense process of the revelation."[1] The revelation, as we know, is that of the victim mechanism that dominates the natural notion of the sacred. This mechanism was first exposed in the Judeo-Christian Scriptures, and Jesus brought the revelation to completion by reinterpreting the apparently victimary passages of the Old Testament in a non-victimary sense as well. But the reason that it is only today that we are in a position to understand in a completely clear way the meaning of Jesus's non-victimary reinterpretation of the Old Testament is also profoundly connected to the specific historical situation of modernity. In fact, the non-victimary reading of the Scripture was already there in the original teachings of Jesus, but, as the Vulgate text of John 1:5 has it, "et lux in tenebris lucet, et tenebrae eam non comprehenderunt." The light—of life, flowing from the *word/verbum/logos*—shines in the darkness and the darkness could not comprehend it. Now, though, the modern dissolution of all traditional (victimary) mechanisms of recomposition of the mimetic rivalry, which has set free the plurality and the explicit conflictuality of desire (I refer again to *Things Hidden*), along with the development of new technical devices of mass destruction have created a situation in which the victimary violence of human culture becomes totally visible and boundless and for the same reason no longer viable. In the present situation of our civilization, Girard thinks, one is faced with a radical alternative: either the complete self-destruction of humankind or the full realization of the charity preached by Jesus.

It is on this basis—the fact that the historical development of modernity has brought about the final unmasking of the victimary mechanism of human culture—that even Heidegger belongs to the history of the revelation. What I want to suggest is that this relation between Heidegger and the history of revelation is more specific than Girard seems to think. Heidegger is not only a part of the scene depicted by Girard; his explicit depiction of the scene is very similar to that of Girard, so similar that his philosophy can be described as an active (not purely unconscious or symptomatic) revelation of the same victimary mechanism that Girard makes us discover in the Judeo-Christian Scripture. In other words, I would suggest that Heidegger's philosophy is (interpretable as) a sort of philosophical, more or less conscious, transcription of the Judeo-Christian revelation.

Consider the analogy between the apocalyptic view of modernity that Girard gives in *Things Hidden* and the accomplishment of metaphysics as Heidegger describes it in his late works. For both Girard and Heidegger, what is decisive and apocalyptic, meaning revelatory, in the present situation is the explosion of violence caused by the fact that in our time the will to power—or the mimetic rivalry—has become explicit and boundless. This explosion makes clear, for Girard, the basic victimary structure of all human culture; for Heidegger, it exposes the "secret" of metaphysics, which is the forgetting of Being and the identification of it with beings, objectivity, etc. The analogy between these two theories becomes evident if we consider that what motivates Heidegger's rejection of metaphysics is not a theoretical reason, as if metaphysics were a false description of Being for which we had to substitute a more adequate one. Heidegger's rejection of metaphysics, as is clear already in *Sein und Zeit*, is motivated by the violence by which it reduces Being—and particularly human existence—to measurable objectivity and rationalized mechanisms. (By the way, one might suggest that even the violence that Heidegger sees involved in the *logos* of both Heraclitus and the Johannine gospel, although in different ways, is the violence of metaphysics that thought has to overcome.)[2]

The most decisive reason to read Heidegger's philosophy as deeply related to Judeo-Christian scripture is, of course (but this is not so often remarked), his notion of Being as *Ereignis*, event, a notion which is an immediate consequence of the unmasking of the oblivion inflicted by metaphysics. It may not be a random fact that while preparing *Sein und Zeit* in the early 1920s, Heidegger was also intensely engaged in reading the New Testament and the writings of Luther. This means, in my view, that in addition to the avant-garde spirit of the beginning of the century (the same one you find emblematically expressed by Ernst Bloch in *Geist der Utopie*), themes and questions arising from his meditation on the problems of grace, freedom, predestination, and so on also helped to prompt his critique and rejection of the objectivism of metaphysics. The overcoming of metaphysics—which in Heidegger's view, as readers probably know, can only be a *Verwindung*,[3] an acceptance-distortion—will prepare a new way of conceiving Being that might also reopen the possibility for religious experience, leaving behind all the metaphysical contradictions that prevent modern reason from seriously heeding the Scriptures (including the difficulty of thinking such notions as creation, sin, salvation, etc.). I don't wish to ignore the fact that Heidegger himself didn't develop this aspect of his thought, and that may be an aspect of what Girard calls the expulsion of the Judeo-Christian text from his philosophy. As I pointed out before, Girard doesn't take this expulsion as a reason for excluding Heidegger from the history of revelation. On the same basis—of what we can consider the "objective" historical meaning of Heidegger's philosophy, no matter what his conscious intentions were—I think we should take the "notion" of Being as event as the philosophical expression of his "reception" of the Judeo-Christian message. One may, of course, speculate on why all this is not visible in Heidegger's explicit self-interpretation. "Et tenebrae eum non comprehenderunt." Even his participation in the Nazi movement is the effect of a philosophical self-misunderstanding on Heidegger's part; the same happens, I think, with his expulsion of the Judeo-Christian tradition from his philosophical discourse. One can probably cite psychological and biographical reasons for this, related both to his need to distance himself from his Catholic origins and the increasing importance in his imagination of a "direct" relation between modern Germany and ancient Greece (an idea that was also one of the elements of his Nazism).

The conception of Being as event is merely a starting point for recognizing the deep kinship (I don't have a more precise term) between Heidegger's philosophy and the Bible. Another aspect of his philosophy appears more important and meaningful, however, and seems more strongly related to Girard's notion of the revelation and dissolution of the violence of the sacred. I am now describing, although not in merely autobiographical terms, the way in which I came to recognize a "completion" of Heidegger in Girard, and also to reinterpret Girard through Heidegger. Everything depends on an effort to be faithful to the basic purpose of Heidegger's philosophy, even against Heidegger himself. The purpose is not so strange: as a matter of fact, in the interpretation of a work of art or of any other text, we usually assume such an attitude. I can here make only a cursory allusion to Luigi Pareyson's theory of the distinction between what (in his *Aesthetics*, 1954)[4] he called *forma formata* and *forma formante*. The evaluation of a work of art, so went Pareyson's thesis, cannot depend on the application of preexisting general criteria (this comes directly from Kant's *Critique of Judgment*). It must be possible to evaluate the work on the basis of the law that it itself wants to institute. And besides: if we don't exclude externally preexisting criteria, we wouldn't be able to explain why the artist revises the work again and again. In both cases, in the evaluative and in the formative processes, we must recognize that what is operative in the work is a rule that is given with the work itself, even where the work doesn't succeed in being what it "wanted" to be. I recall this theory of Pareyson's because, as Gadamer also recognizes in *Truth and Method*, it outlines an analysis of the act of interpretation that is not to be found in much of contemporary hermeneutics. What Pareyson says of the aesthetic experience seems to me perfectly applicable to the interpretation of a philosophical work, and probably to every act of interpretation.

The *forma formante* of Heidegger's critique of metaphysics, which is the effort to think Being no longer in terms of an ultimate foundation, objectivity, stability, and so on, seems to me to legitimate what I propose to call a left-wing interpretation of Heidegger's philosophy, as opposed to what, with reference to the history of the Hegelian school in the nineteenth century, can be called the right-wing interpretation of it. From this point of view, Heidegger's notion of ontological difference can be taken seriously only if one rejects the idea that Being *is* something—subtracted from our possible experience, like the God of negative theology, but nevertheless objectively "given" somewhere else, beyond all names by which we might call him. In order to avoid this extreme regression into a metaphysical identification of Being with objective presence, a postmetaphysical philosophy has to be ready to think the event of Being in terms of an indefinite type of ongoing subtraction, a weakening, a taking-leave, or long farewell. (In a page of the late *Zeit und Sein* Heidegger says that a nonmetaphysical thinking must "let Being, as the foundation of that which exists, go" ["das Sein als den Grund des Seienden fahren zu lassen"], let it depart, let it take its leave).[5] It is not coincidental that to indicate nonmetaphysical thought (*Denken*) Heidegger uses the word *An-denken*, rememoration: a rememoration that does not intend to re-present Being again because this would amount to a pure and simple restoration of metaphysics (along with its violence). Being can only be authentically thought as "receding." Is there a reminiscence here of the image of God being seen by Moses only from the back, while going away?

The further step that can lead (that can lead me, at any rate) to a linking of Heidegger and Girard is to emphasize—beyond the letter of Heidegger's texts—the trait of weakening that characterizes, in this hypothesis, the event of Being. Being eventuates—from time to time, in its historical-destinal apertures (which can roughly but usefully be compared to Thomas Kuhn's paradigms)—only as ontological difference, that is, as the disruption of the pretensions, of the claims of beings to definitiveness, stability, ultimacy. (On this specific point, readers are referred to Reiner Schürmann's *Heidegger on Being and Acting*.)[6] Being is the very principle of weakening. Modernity, in its dissolutionary aspects—the dissolution of authoritarian political institutions; the dissolution of the belief in the ultimacy of consciousness; the dissolution of the very notion of reality through a multiplication of, and explicit conflict among, the different agencies of interpretation interacting in our society, and also through the increasing historical self-consciousness of the sciences—is not a purely negative preparation for the final accomplishment of the revelation. If modernity makes it impossible to still believe in the victimary mechanism, it belongs positively to the history of salvation.

Seen in these terms, the weakening of Being as its sole form of manifesting itself beyond metaphysical oblivion, is an analogon of the dissolution of the violence of the sacred, which, for Girard, is the meaning of the Judeo-Christian Scripture. *Kénosis* is probably the word best suited to connect these two discourses, which are apparently so different. For both Girard and Heidegger, the emancipatory meaning of history—the salvation that takes place in it—is related to a self-consumption of the violence that characterizes natural religion or, in Heidegger, the metaphysical oblivion of Being.

As I said above, I am perfectly well aware that this reading of Heidegger through Girard involves not only strong choices about the meaning of Heidegger's texts (what I call left-wing Heideggerianism, which I have discussed more extensively elsewhere), but also a reinterpretation of Girard that he may not accept. The delicate point seems to me to reside in the fact that Girard, in the last analysis, does not wish to speak in terms of the "history of Being," as Heidegger does; rather, he wants to offer a "scientific" anthropology. That's why, rather astonishingly, the third book of *Things Hidden* is devoted to "interindividual psychology," as if (I exaggerate, but not all that much) the entire historical process that developed from the primitive mechanism of the scapegoat to biblical revelation and to the incarnation of Christ had the sole aim of finally preparing the possibility of a scientific, nonvictimary knowledge of human nature. I know that this is not Girard's intention, but as a matter of fact, even the redemptive power of Jesus seems to reside, for him, in a pure and simple theoretical unmasking of the violent essence of the natural notion of the sacred. This, of course, is strategically decisive in putting today's humankind in the condition of being obliged to choose between violence and Christian love, but this, apparently, is all. What about the notion of grace, of the salvation that is inherently related to the incarnation of Jesus Christ? Girard, of course, wants to avoid any return to the victimary reading of Jesus's story, but this seems to lead him too far afield, so that redemption runs the risk of becoming a mere matter of knowledge.

What I am suggesting, very sketchily and roughly here, is that the revelation of the connection between the sacred and violence happens along with, and only by means of, the incarnation of Christ, through the *kénosis*. This means, in my view, that salvation is not primarily a matter of consciousness that faces us with an ineluctable choice between violent mimetic rivalry and charity; rather, it is the announcement that God saves us through a historical process of education that is, at the same time, a revelation and a progressive reduction of the original violence of the sacred. Salvation is the historical process through which God calls us, time and again, to desacralize the violence and dissolve the ultimacy and peremptoriness claimed by objectivist metaphysics. This process has no end; it is certainly not ended by the revelation of an apocalyptic alternative between total violence and perfect charity. By the way, Girard seems to think that the history of salvation, and the non-victimary reinterpretation of Scripture, terminates with the episode of Emmaus (see the conclusion of the second book of *Things Hidden*). Should he not also take into account the story of the descent of the Holy Spirit—which inaugurates the reinterpretation of Scripture by the living community of the church?

Along these lines, which necessarily remain simple outlines here, I think that Girard himself, or at least (some of) his readers, ought to reconsider the possibility of developing a more than merely polemical dialogue between the decisive discovery of the victimary mechanism and the end of metaphysics that Heidegger tried to effect.

René Girard

FACTS, INTERPRETATIONS

From the standpoint of "deconstructive nihilism," modern atheism is only one "metaphysical" creed among many others. The reassurance provided by its supposedly scientific grounding is as illusory as the reassurance of religions, philosophies, and ideologies. A complete liberation from false certainties demands that atheism be deconstructed too, along with other metaphysical illusions. Once this task is accomplished, Christianity should become attractive once again. In a genuinely "nihilistic" world, the religion of the cross should fare better than all the creeds and ideologies that imprudently relied on false scientific "objectivity." This is what Gianni Vattimo suggests in his recent works, notably *Belief* and, a little before that, *Beyond Interpretation*:

> Contemporary hermeneutics seems to be only, or above all, a theory that frees reason from its slavery to the scientistic ideal of objectivity, only to pave the way to a philosophy of culture whose limits (and meaning) cannot ultimately be determined. *Having dissolved the metaphysical idea of truth as conformity (primarily thanks to Heidegger), hermeneutics*

lends fresh plausibility to religion and even myth, quite independently of any Hegelian style historicist justification.[1]

Christianity values human reason but does not believe it can lead to some absolute truth. The Nietzschean-Heideggerian school disdainfully dismisses as "metaphysical" and "ontotheological" the rational systems elaborated by theologians. But ordinary Christians have never confused these systems with the redemptive power of the cross. They rely not on philosophy but on *faith*, *hope*, and *charity*. Sooner or later, therefore, the opposition to Christianity should weaken. The first signs of such weakening should appear where they are least expected, among the radical intellectuals who understand best the nihilistic implications of their philosophy. Is Vattimo himself such a sign?

In recent years, this philosopher has drawn closer once again to the Catholic Church of his youth. This evolution may shock some of his fellow deconstructionists who have not sufficiently plumbed the depth of their own nihilism. Vattimo does not seem unduly concerned. In *Beyond Interpretation*, he observes that his recent work "leads in a direction that might be seen as scandalous, in that it 'twists' weakness and nihilism into a sense totally different to the usual; and above all because it ends somehow in the arms of theology—albeit in ways that do not bring it into contact with any 'orthodoxy.'"[2] The words "weakness and nihilism" are references to the attitude that Vattimo advocates as *pensiero debole*, the "weakening" or "softening" of all "structures of Being." Vattimo does not define his religious evolution in the classic terms of a Christian conversion. He sees it as a fulfillment rather than a recantation of his nihilism. The Church of today is different, of course, from the one he left. Since Vatican II, many things have changed, not as radically perhaps as one might wish but sufficiently to justify this re-orientation. Vattimo hopes for a total elimination of attitudes that he regards as vestiges from the past, the refusal to ordain women, for instance, and the condemnation of homosexual practices.

Vattimo often sounds like one of those Catholics whom American traditionalists call "cafeteria Catholics." In the doctrine of the Church, they pick and choose what they like and they leave out the rest. The idea that Catholicism is an all-or-nothing proposition has disappeared. Accurate as it is literally, this characterization fails to capture the spirit of Vattimo's writing, which is entirely positive and conveys a real love for the Church. The contrast with the *ressentiment* of current debates, on both sides of the fence, is refreshing. Resentful Catholics, more often than not, are Catholics on their way out of the Church; Vattimo is a Catholic on his way back in, and that makes a world of difference. So does his peculiar talent for thinking vigorously without losing his serenity. His main religious theme is the divine *kénosis*, the "debilist" side of God, one might say, which does not exclude strong incarnational and trinitarian overtones. Vattimo may not be as alien to orthodoxy as his language implies.

His recent books tend to attribute the aspects of the Church he condemns to historical factors, to the prolonged inability of Christianized pagans to renounce the violent *sacred* embodied in the archaic (or as he calls them, "natural") religions. In connection with this idea, Vattimo summarizes my work as follows:

> Girard, we recall here in the briefest of terms, sees the natural religions as founded on a victim-based conception of the sacred: when serious conflicts break out within the community, the way to heal them is to concentrate on a single

(sacrificial) scapegoat the violence that would otherwise be unleashed against everyone. Since the scapegoat functions effectively to reduce the violence, it assumes a sacral and divine character. The meaning of the Old and the New Testaments, however, is to reveal the falsehood of the sacred as violent and natural. Jesus, most especially, comes to be put to death not because he is the perfect victim, as has always been understood, but because he is the bearer of a message too radically in contrast with the deepest (sacral and victim-based) convictions of all the "natural religions." The extraordinary character of his revelation (the sacred is not sacrificial violence, God is Love) demonstrates, amongst other things, that he could not be only human.[3]

From this remarkable summary, Vattimo draws many inferences with which I agree and some with which I disagree. I agree, of course, with his condemnation of all the violence that, in the past, was committed, authorized, or tolerated by the Church. I also agree, evidently, with the principle of free interpretation, with the refusal to treat the Bible differently from any other text.

Vattimo explicitly sides with the so-called progressive or liberal trends that, since Vatican II, have become dominant almost everywhere at the local and national levels in the Catholic Church. This choice has deep roots in his intellectual and religious past. One of his first books was a study of Schleiermacher, the founding father of liberal Protestantism.[4] The word that sums up the evolution he finds positive is "secularization": "this movement [toward 'secularization'] is helped along by René Girard's theories on violence and the sacred—even if he does not himself push them as far as these conclusions (and at bottom it is not clear why not)."[5] It goes without saying for Vattimo that my writing necessarily leads to the position he advocates. I myself believe that it leads to a confirmation not of all past practices of the Church, to be sure, but of the traditional orthodoxy.

There is a misunderstanding between us, and it has several causes. One of these is obvious, and I am 100 percent responsible for it. In *Things Hidden Since the Foundation of the World* (first published in 1978), I decided not to use the word "sacrifice" in conjunction with the cross.[6] This decision has most probably influenced Vattimo's estimation of my work. Like many readers, he interprets my past rejection of the word "sacrifice" as a repudiation of orthodoxy that I did not really intend. For more than ten years, before focusing on Christianity, I had studied with great intensity the blood sacrifices of the archaic or natural religions. My attitude toward sacrifice has remained indelibly marked by this experience. In blood sacrifice, the sacrificers inflict violence upon their victims. This is a far cry, obviously, from what we call the sacrifice of Christ, which is the crucifixion. Jesus does not inflict violence on anybody but, on the contrary, suffers it himself for a purpose that, whatever its definition, has nothing to do with inflicting violence on any living creature. The primary significance of sacrifice, the violence inflicted by the sacrificers, dominates most of mankind's history, and unquestionably it reappears as a metaphor in some Christian theories of redemption. Because of their indifference to archaic religions, Christian thinkers rarely investigate the relationship between blood sacrifices and what they call the sacrifice of Christ. As a result, they cannot effectively confront the modern tendency to associate the two for the purpose of dismissing Christianity as "one more sacrificial myth."

For my part, after studying archaic sacrifice, I was and I remain so impressed with the discontinuity between its archaic modalities and the sacrifice of Christ that, in order to place maximum emphasis on the opposition, I simply rejected the use of the word for the Christian cross. A few years later, thanks in large measure to Raymund Schwager, I realized that this solution is untenable, or rather it is no solution at all, if only because the symbolic symmetry between archaic sacrifice and the cross cannot be meaningless from a Christian standpoint. The attachment of orthodox theologians to certain traditional *words*, such as "sacrifice," even if it still needs to be explored, is never without reason. Even though we must vigorously oppose the confusion between archaic sacrifice and the sacrifice of Christ, a rejection of the word itself leads to a sterile denial of history in the *geschichtlich* sense. Christ accepts being sacrificed against all blood sacrifices, and his gift of himself, paradoxical as it may seem, must ultimately be defined, I now believe, in terms of (self)-sacrifice.

I used to believe, like Vattimo, that the use of the old sacrificial language and the definition of Jesus as the "perfect victim" prevented a real understanding of the Passion as fully "antisacrificial," but I now think I was wrong. My rejection of the word "sacrifice" was, for the most part, an honest mistake. And yet it was also prompted in part, no doubt, by the old desire to twist the aged lion's tail and loudly *disagree* with the Church, just for the sake of disagreeing. I was trying to redeem myself somewhat in the eyes of fellow intellectuals. For three hundred years, all of us intellectuals have chained ourselves to *la révolte*, and the addiction is hard to break. Now that *la révolte* has reached even the Catholic clergy the end of this particular tunnel must be in sight! In an essay published in 1995 entitled "The Mimetic Theory and Theology," I rejected my former rejection of the word "sacrifice."[7] This short piece, however, fails to answer most of the questions raised by the issue. My most recent book says nothing on the subject either.[8] I hope to return to it in the future, and I apologize for saying so little.

The second cause of the misunderstanding between Vattimo and me is our different attitudes toward interpretation. He does not realize, I feel, how old-fashioned I am on this subject compared to him. To define what he calls his "nihilistic hermeneutics," Vattimo often quotes an excerpt from a famous aphorism found in Nietzsche's late notebooks: "Against the positivism which halts at phenomena—'There are only facts'—I would say: no, facts are just what there aren't, there are only interpretations."[9] This sentence is a brilliant piece of polemic against the vetero-positivists who felt that each time they opened their mouths an immortal scientific truth would leap out of it. But Nietzsche's boutade cannot provide a functional theory of interpretation. To have nothing but interpretations is the same as having none. Most of the time, Nietzsche disregards his own formula and, with all due respect, the same is true of Vattimo himself, I feel, quite fortunately for his readers. The people who take the fashionable ostracizing of facts too seriously end up sounding like the politically correct academics they effectively are.

The Nietzschean slogan plays into the hands of those who turn all texts into insipid "narratives" or more or less fictional "stories" that are not supposed to make sense except independently from one another. The comparative analyses I pursue are meaningless unless the mythical and the biblical make sense together and therefore can significantly oppose each other. The Nietzschean denial of facts has a semblance of plausibility only with philosophers and poets intent on generating as many interpretations as possible from a subject matter as tenuous as possible. Mallarmé's *aboli bibelot d'inanité sonore* was more than a game to Mallarmé himself, no doubt, but, after Mallarmé, what else can it be?

There is nothing Mallarmean about the interpretive sequence that dominates my work: it is terribly commonsensical and down-to-earth, disgustingly referential. It rests on the obvious, and it seeks the obvious. Not everything obvious interests me, to be sure, only those observations that should have been made long ago and yet never were. Our relationship to the Gospels, I feel, is full of unacknowledged obviousness. In order to show how alien to the sophisticated nihilism of our time my interpretive practice is, I will summarize once again my main reasoning, just to emphasize its theoretical rusticity.

THE SCAPEGOAT

Even casual readers are aware that the crucifixion results from the collaboration of many people, an entire mob really, which has become hostile to Jesus quite suddenly and "without a cause." In the more spectacular dramas of the Old Testament, we also find a great deal of violence either indirectly collective, as in the crucifixion, or quite directly, and then it can only be defined as lynching, as in the case of the "suffering servant" (Isaiah 53:7), or the many prophets who suffer and even die at the hands of hostile mobs. What about mythology? The collective violence that I have just noted in the two testaments obviously plays a major role in mythology as well. The most archaic myths, in particular, are full of lynching. The descriptions of this violence are not as graphic as in Isaiah or in the Gospels but they are simply too numerous to be ignored. They are even more numerous than it seems since, in some myths where, at first sight, collective violence seems absent, comparative analyses suggest that *it has been suppressed.*[10] As in the Gospels and in the Bible, in mythology the ganging up of many assailants against a single victim occurs at the climax of a community-wide crisis and, as a rule, puts an end to that crisis. These similarities cannot be fortuitous. Behind all the lynching there must be a cause that transcends individual situations. Myths contain no useful information on the subject, but the Gospels do. They show that it is not merely the enemies of Jesus or the people indifferent to him who succumb to the violent impulse, but his very friends, his dearest disciples, Peter himself. The contagion of violence is so powerful that it does not spare even those who share Jesus' sufferings, the two thieves crucified next to him (one only in Luke). Even though already nailed to their own crosses, they still want to become crucifiers; they desperately want to belong to the lynching mob. The Gospels never suggest that this contagious violence might be divine, just the opposite. It is rooted in the mimetic nature of human relations, which is divisive most of the time but which, at its paroxysm, may suddenly become unitive and solidify an entire community against a single victim. Human divisiveness can suddenly become the strange and terrifying glue of human communities.

To designate this never fully understood phenomenon, we resort, unthinkingly, to a biblical word, "scapegoat," which originally designates the victim of a ritual described in Leviticus 16. The modern world has deritualized and broadened its meaning. "Scapegoating" designates the process of violent contagion that we can still observe everywhere in our world, most of the time but not always in an attenuated form. The language of the gospels confirms the scapegoat interpretation of Jesus' death: one of the titles given to him, "the lamb of God," is synonymous with "scapegoat" and is occasionally used in that sense among us, mostly by Christians unafraid to suggest that our understanding of collective persecution must come from the Gospels. Another indication that Jesus dies the death of a scapegoat is the presence, in two Gospels out of four, of a second or rather a first scapegoat episode that, in many respects, duplicates the crucifixion: the murder of John the Baptist. It takes only one executioner to decapitate John, no doubt, but many people share in the responsibility for his death: Salome, Herod, Herodias, and all the dinner guests of Herod who play the same role as the crowd in the crucifixion. They put pressure on Herod by asking for the prophet's head.

What about myths? Ought we to interpret their innumerable lynchings and other instances of collective and quasi-collective violence as "scapegoating" as well? It seems reasonable to think so. Since the textual data are the same, the facts behind them should be the same. And yet, far from verifying this conjecture, myths spectacularly contradict it. Instead of seeing in them the same innocent victims as the two testaments portray, they represent these victims as culprits justly condemned for offenses they have really committed. The biblical pattern is reversed in the case of the victims, and it is reversed in the case of the persecutors as well. Instead of irrational mobs that turn violent without a cause, many myths represent orderly citizens who do resort to violence, no doubt, but for legitimate reasons: they must save their community. The Oedipus tragedy is a good example. The hero is certainly not a scapegoat *from the standpoint of his own myth*: he really has committed the parricide and incest of which he is accused. The Thebans have not only the right but the duty to remove him from his throne and cast him into outer darkness.

If we compare the biblical and the mythical patterns, we can see that the beliefs of the mobs and their violence are the same everywhere, but the interpretation is different. Whereas myths espouse uncritically the beliefs of their own violent mobs, the Old and New Testaments denounce these same mobs and side with the victims. When we shift from the mythical to the biblical, everything remains structurally identical, but the distribution of guilt and innocence inside that structure is systematically reversed. Does this reversal mean that the word "scapegoat" is applicable only to the Old and New Testaments and not to mythology? Just the opposite: it means that scapegoating is essential only to the definition of mythology.

Is this an empty paradox? If we reflect on the significance of the scapegoat and scapegoating, we will see that it is not. How does the violent contagion of scapegoating influence the scapegoaters? It convinces them that their victim is guilty. Since the persecutors truly believe something that is not true, what else can they do when they report their experience but to state this untruth as if it were the truth? In view of its structural similarities with the great dramas in the Old and New Testament, mythology must consist in accounts of scapegoating that are systematically misleading not because they try to deceive but because the authors themselves are deceived. They do not intentionally lie. They do not try to fool us: they themselves are fooled. They really perceive in their victims the horrendous culprits they portray. They are imprisoned in the illusion of scapegoating. When the experience of scapegoating is really "perfect," when the violent contagion is so powerful that all dissent disappears, it can only generate what we call mythology. This definition makes it possible to understand the religious dimension of myths. Unanimous scapegoating effectively transfers to the victim all the societal tensions and aggressions that divide the scapegoaters, and it truly reconciles them. In other words it puts an end to the crisis with which all accounts of scapegoating begin.

The scapegoaters are humbly aware that they themselves cannot be responsible for their reconciliation, and they attribute it to its only possible cause in the context of their total experience, the scapegoat once again. That is why, in the end, an effective scapegoat is necessarily perceived as a divinity who came down incognito from heaven to visit the community. The mysterious visitor treats the people very harshly at first but ultimately rescues them from all harm. That is the reason archaic scapegoats are regarded as divine saviors, divine ancestors, or full-fledged divinities. When scapegoating is most intense and unanimous, the victim is perceived first as a dreadful malefactor and then, after the unanimous violence, as an all-powerful benefactor who presides over the reconstruction of the community and, above all, teaches the people how to perform ritual sacrifices. These must obviously be defined as the deliberate repetition of the original scapegoating with substitute victims, for the dual purpose of honoring the god and reactivating the "purifying" or *cathartic* energy of unanimous scapegoating.

Scapegoating is a most paradoxical and invisible phenomenon, the revelation of which is humanly impossible. The impossibility is why, even today, most people cannot understand its role in human culture. Either the mimetic contagion is unanimous and it generates a myth that conceals its own origin, or the contagion is too weak to be unanimous and scapegoating does not occur at all. The real problem for anthropologists is not mythology, which is relatively easy to explain, but the infinitely mysterious presence among us of one religious tradition and one only, the Judaic and the Christian, that, instead of being rooted

109

RENÉ GIRARD

in scapegoating and keeping it concealed, literally "unconceals" it. Thus the foundational experience of Christianity is scapegoating once again, *which makes it both inseparable from all other religions and incomparable with them.*

In the Passion, we immediately recognize in Jesus an innocent victim, a scapegoat. The real reason for the convergence of many persecutors against him, the mimetic contagion of violence, is publicly exhibited. Whereas in mythology scapegoating is transfigured into the just punishment of a culprit and therefore concealed, in the gospels the disgraceful truth is portrayed as it really is. Archaic religions seem totally alien to scapegoating not because they are so but for the opposite reason. They are scapegoating itself, so pure and unadulterated that it cannot portray itself as scapegoating. All we need do in order to understand what myths really are is to read them as Passion accounts distorted by the persecutors. According to Francis Goyet, this is what the Byzantine Empire did in the case of Sophocles' *Oedipus Rex*. It insisted not upon the sensational discovery of the hero's mythical guilt but upon the hero's sufferings. The tragedy was read as the Passion of Oedipus.[11] Those who regard Judaism and Christianity as *the* religions of scapegoating, because scapegoating becomes visible in them, blame the messenger for the message and do not understand the difference between the principle of illusion that scapegoating is, and the accurate representation of it, which dissipates the illusion. The religions of scapegoating were those in which scapegoating was not represented and therefore remained effective in many different ways.

For my scapegoat thesis to be true, it must fit not just some mythical data but all of them. This essay is too brief, of course, for an exhaustive investigation, but I will enumerate now a few characteristics of mythical heroes and heroines that indirectly confirm the foundational role of scapegoating in structuring mythology. If mythical heroes have nothing to do with the stereotyped crimes attributed to them (parricide, incest, and the rest), why were certain individuals selected rather than other members of the community? In many cases, there is nothing in the myths that can suggest an answer, but in other myths there is. Many heroes present features that are not truly characteristic of their individual "identities," since they keep recurring in many myths, but that are suggestive of their identity as victims. They possess attributes that, in a provincial and primitive community, may earmark them for mistreatment and persecution. It is something trivial and yet significant, even in our own world, since we recognize this significance. Many mythical heroes are sick, crippled, or afflicted with infirmities and abnormalities that, sad to say, are likely to trigger the hostility of their neighbors against them. The number of mythical heroes who limp or who have lost an eye, an arm, or a leg, is enormous. Others present peculiarities that, even today, would severely try the patience of their neighbors. They emit a foul smell, for instance, which accounts for their being ultimately divinized since it is the reason they are victimized. Other heroes are so poor that they are reduced to begging. Others still are horribly ugly or, on the contrary, are so amazingly privileged in terms of wealth, physical strength, personal charm, and so on that they must arouse a jealousy that may well be the primary cause of scapegoating. In isolated and highly "provincial" communities, something else is likely to cause persecution: the lack of adaptation that comes as a result of foreignness. All over the world, divine ancestors, heroes, demigods, or gods are often defined as visiting strangers when they first show up in the community that becomes polarized against them.

I have just enumerated a few *preferential signs* or *stereo-types* of victimization, and the list could go on indefinitely.[12] Many victims have no sign, to be sure, but the fact does not refute my thesis. In scapegoating there is an element of randomness that defeats all attempts at exhaustive enumeration and infallible pre-diction. That element of uncertainty does not diminish the sci-entific nature of this type of investigation. Clues are scattered here and there, but there are just too many of them, and there are too many myths, for any doubt to remain regarding the true nature of mythology and ritual: it is the religious transfiguration of a scapegoating forever concealed as a result.

Highly relevant in the present context is another group of ac-cusations, ones that seem deliberately tailored to scapegoating. Some heroes are accused of having devised some trick in order to cause dissension among the members of a troubled community. Cadmus, the founding hero of Theban mythology, is accused of covertly throwing a stone in the midst of giants in order to arouse their anger and engineer their mutual destruction. We find something similar in Germanic-Scandinavian mythology, in the figure of Wotan. In a South American myth studied by Lévi-Strauss (in his *Mythologiques*), an invisible parrot, hidden high in the branches of a tree, is supposed to cast twigs at some warriors down below—once again for the purpose of triggering their mutual destruction. Such stories are not full-blown myths, but there is something mythical in them since they must be in-vented after the fact, as a face-saving device that allows the sur-vivors to make peace. They could be defined, perhaps, in terms of "conflict-resolution devices." The same is true, I believe, of many *trickster* pranks.[13] Some must be deliberately fabricated in order to deflect dangerous anger toward a third party who may be real in some cases, imaginary in others. Spectacular troublemakers often are reconcilers in disguise, in the sense that they assume responsibility for all provocative behavior.

Many mythical victims are accused, of course, of horrendous crimes such as parricide, incest, bestiality, and similar monstrosities. In order to detect the scapegoat nature of these crimes we must remember that they often reappear, as slanderous accusations, in instances of collective persecution still occurring in our historical world, or recent enough to be unmistakable. Our tincture of Christianity gives us an intelligence of scapegoating far superior to that of any other world and forbids misreading these persecutions as the unfathomably profound and charming myths we would certainly see in them if we had discovered them in a Greek or archaic context. Until now, our professional mythologists have refused to project our modern scapegoat insight back into the Greek world. One must take not just the single *Schritt zurück* to the pre-Socratic philosophers advocated by Heidegger, but a second one, back to the mythical violence that will reveal the true origins of our culture. These origins will turn out to be the same as the cross, but misunderstood. There are signs that our enforced blindness is about to collapse.

THE VICTIMARY MECHANISM

The scapegoat hypothesis is really a double one. It shows that myths make sense as the concealment of a scapegoating that gradually becomes unconcealed in the Old and New Testaments. We must now look at the Passion again for more signs that it really unconceals scapegoating. The main clue is the presence in the crucifixion accounts of something totally absent from mythology, a group of unbelievers in scapegoating. Next to the loyal scapegoaters, who remain the largest group by far, we have a dissident minority, Jesus' apostles. This minority is indispensable, obviously, to the unconcealment of scapegoating. Its existence is not something to be taken for granted. The loyal scapegoaters must still dominate the scene, or there would be no concealed scapegoating. If belief in the victim's guilt were limited to a minority or a weak majority, even if the victim was killed, the whole process would not be concealed sufficiently to be effective. There would be no genuine scapegoating to unconceal. The scapegoating must be powerful enough to succeed as scapegoating, but it must not be so powerful that it will make dissent impossible. The scapegoating of Jesus satisfies these two conditions. A dissenting minority must have been present as well in the case of the Old Testament dramas that unconceal scapegoating, but, contrary to what happens in the Gospels, it remains invisible.

Myths, as a rule, contain no dissenting minority. The official truth of scapegoating is never challenged. I know only one exception to that rule, the story of Romulus's death in Livy (1.16.4). Romulus stands on top of one of Rome's seven hills, surrounded by the entire Senate. Suddenly a big storm occurs, and a cloud hides everybody. When the fog lifts, Romulus is gone, and the senators announce to the assembled people that he has been taken straight to heaven. The people dutifully rejoice except for some nasty individuals who claim that that they saw some senators carrying pieces of Romulus's body away under their togas. The report is dismissed as the invention of unreliable malcontents.

Immediately before and during the crucifixion the apostles are far from immune to the contagion of scapegoating. At the crucial moment, therefore, the prospect for the emergence of a dissenting minority is bleak. If all the disciples had surrendered for good to scapegoating, there would have been no Gospels.

If the crucifixion had been recorded at all, it could have been recorded only in mythical form. It is the resurrection of Jesus that brings the dissenting minority into being, at a time when, humanly speaking, the truth had been buried with him once and for all. The resurrection is attributed to the Spirit of God, aptly named the Paraclete, a word that signifies the lawyer for the defense. The resurrection shows that scapegoating is a prison from which the apostles would never have broken free without divine help. The Paraclete enables the disciples to perceive something no human being can perceive without its help, his own individual participation in scapegoating. This awareness is one with the process we call Christian conversion, and it plays a spectacular role among the apostles around the time of the resurrection, especially in the case of Peter after his denial, and later of Paul on the road to Damascus. Paul did not understand his own violence until he heard from Jesus' own mouth a most amazing question: "Saul, Saul, why are you persecuting me?" (Acts 9:3–7). A scapegoat anthropology can take us very far, no doubt, but beyond this point it cannot go. It must give way to religion. The universality of the scapegoat pattern in religious texts suggests that all human societies are afflicted with some kind of malfunction that, even though fully revealed in the Gospels, has always escaped the attention of scientific observers as well as of Christian thinkers themselves.

The cause of this malfunction can only be mankind's enormous capacity for conflict. It would have made human societies impossible if, in our pre-Christian history, whenever the disorder crossed a certain threshold of intensity, it did not spontaneously trigger its own antidote in the form of some unanimous scapegoating that generated not only mythology and the archaic notion of the sacred, but ritual sacrifices, thus providing human societies with sacrificial means to keep violence in check. If scapegoat religions did truly protect mankind from its own violence, then the Gospel revelation of scapegoating is really a most momentous and dangerous change in the course of human history. As this revelation gradually spread to all of mankind, it liberated both our creative and destructive capacities.

The contrast between the positive and optimistic conclusions of myths and the apocalyptic dimension of Judeo-Christianity is one more clue, I think, in favor of ascribing both the similarities and dissimilarities between them to scapegoating, which remains forever concealed in the first and becomes unconcealed in the second. In myths, the concealment makes scapegoating effective. The old system returns, or a new one replaces it, and that is why mythical conclusions are positive and optimistic. A cultural restoration or a new instauration is taking place under the supervision of the newly revealed god, who is none other than the annihilated scapegoat. The Gospels are different. The goodness of their good news depends on all of us abiding by the rules of the kingdom of God. If we do not, if we remain vengeful, it will become impossible, at some future time, to restrain the spiraling violence that does not come from God but from unrestrained humanity. Far from being absent from John's Gospel, as claimed by many scholars, the apocalyptic threat is present in the form of all the strife caused by Jesus' interventions, in spite of all the good they accomplish. Jesus' famous sentence, "It is not peace I have come to bring, but a sword" (Matthew 10:34), reflects his awareness that he is destroying the cathartic power of scapegoating and therefore, even though, or rather because he will ultimately give us "that peace of God, which is so much greater than we can understand" (Philippians 4:7), his passage among us must first be followed by a difficult historical transition during which his peace is not yet here and the old peace of the world, in other words the truce of scapegoating, is already gone.

The revelation of the cross brings countless benefits in its wake, no doubt, but as it spreads it deprives human societies of the only kind of peace they enjoyed under the old scapegoat dispensations. In the case of myths, the divine principle is really the violence that brings peace through the mysteries of scapegoating and ritual sacrifice, the good violence that expels the bad one. In the Gospels, this violence is defined not as divine but as satanic. It is the power to "cast out Satan" (Mark 3:23), temporarily given to Satan himself and now withdrawn by Christ. The reason Jesus is regarded as divine is truly unique. His love transcends the violent sacred and, in the end, it must penetrate the dark kingdom of man; it must triumph over all the obstacles we place in the path of our own salvation. In mythical texts as well as in biblical ones, I find many clues to the truth of the scapegoat hypothesis, but the greatest clue is the perfect way in which the two series dovetail. Instead of playing against the Gospels, as they always have so far in the modern world, the similarities between mythology and the Bible will now enable us to vindicate the *intellectual* as well as the religious truth of the two testaments. The four Passion accounts, and the biblical revelations that precede them, are the instruments that can unconceal scapegoating in the texts where it lies concealed, not only in the natural religions but in the philosophies and other modern mythologies such as the social sciences with their mirage of scientific objectivity, justly rejected by Vattimo. A proper application of the mimetic and scapegoating insights provided by the gospels can, so to speak, probe all these texts with X rays.

Before I began to suspect that these possibilities lay within reach, I was interested, like everybody around me, in the various theoretical fashions, including their most antireferential, antilogical and antiscientific modalities. As soon as I became convinced, rightly or wrongly, that scapegoating can play a decisive role in the solution of the mythical-sacrificial riddle, a solution that is really revealed not by me but by the Gospels and thus confirms their unique truth and their unique revelatory power, I sensed a major breakthrough, and I decided to dedicate myself entirely to this insight. Without a backward glance, I renounced all theoretical games, and I returned to the most commonsensical and traditional rules of evidence. I instinctively felt and I still feel that the only theory I need is a belief in the discoverability of the truth—a belief in the existence of both facts and interpretations.

In the search for knowledge, the last century and a half was characterized by excess, first in one direction and then in the other. First there were the schools of thought that worshiped facts and felt so easily and constantly in touch with them that they forgot interpretations. This excess was followed by a reaction in the opposite direction, legitimate in principle but that led almost immediately to excesses worse than the ones they were supposed to rectify. Let us try to renounce all pseudo-*radicalizations*. Let us trust anew in reason but without idolatry. From now on, let us believe in both facts and interpretations.

NOTES

Acknowledgments: My particular thanks go to René Girard and Gianni Vattimo for the mutual openness and good humor they have shown at every one of their encounters and for their concrete assistance in putting this volume together. My thanks go as well to the town council of Falconara and the province of Ancona for having hosted and financed the meeting on "Faith and Relativism," and to Alberto Garlini and the organizing committee of the Pordenonelegge festival for having hosted, and agreed to the publication of, the dialogue on "Christianity and Modernity." Thanks finally to Santiago Zabala and Wendy Lochner for all their help in making the publication of this English translation possible, and to Imitatio for support of the translation.

INTRODUCTION

1. [The adjective *laico* (also a noun), and the nouns *laicismo* and *laicità* (and the French counterparts of these words), have a range of meaning and historical importance in European history that go far beyond the normal range of the English nouns "laicism," "laicity," and "layman" or the adjective "laic." The laity comprised all who were not ordained priests or clerics of some

sort and were therefore outside and beneath the Roman Catholic Church, inasmuch as the Church was a hierarchical priesthood with a vocation to dominate and govern the laity. Historical development in the nineteenth and twentieth centuries caused this group of words to assume meanings ranging from "hostile to the influence of the Catholic hierarchy in the public realm" to "indifferent to religion in the public realm," and that is the range of meanings intended here, and generally in this volume. The terms "secular," "secularism," and "secularization" have a related but distinct meaning. On a straightforward, minimal definition, they denote the growth, over roughly the last five hundred years, of areas of human thought and action, including the sciences and politics, that are governed by their own immanent logics, without religious supervision. But the deeper meanings of the word "secularization" are a topic of discussion between Vattimo and Girard throughout this book.—WM]

2. M. Gauchet, *The Disenchantment of the World*, foreword Charles Taylor, trans. Oscar Burge (Princeton, N.J.: Princeton University Press 1999).

3. See R. Rorty and G. Vattimo, *The Future of Religion*, ed. Santiago Zabala (New York: Columbia University Press, 2005), 72.

4. The dates given in the text are those for the publication of the original Italian editions. The English translations are: *The End of Modernity: Nihilism and Hermeneutics in Postmodern Culture*, trans. Jon R. Snyder (Baltimore, Md.: Johns Hopkins University Press, 1991); *The Transparent Society*, trans. David Webb (Baltimore, Md.: Johns Hopkins University Press, 1994); *After Christianity*, trans. Luca D'Isanto (New York: Columbia University Press, 2002); *Nihilism and Emancipation: Ethics, Politics, and Law*, ed. Santiago Zabala, trans. William McCuaig (New York: Columbia University Press, 2004).

5. R. Girard, *Violence and the Sacred*, trans. Patrick Gregory (Baltimore, Md.: Johns Hopkins University Press, 1977). The date given in the text is that of the publication of the original French edition.

6. Vattimo read *Things Hidden Since the Foundation of the World* in the middle of the 1980s, and first teamed up with Girard in public at Stanford in 1995.

7. Girard has interpreted Nietzsche in light of his own sacrificial theory in various essays: "Superman and the Underground: Strategies of Madness—Nietzsche, Wagner, and Dostoyevsky," *Modern Language Notes* 91 (1976): 1161–85; "Nietzsche and Contradiction," *Stanford Italian Review* 6, no. 1–2 (1986): 53–65; "The Founding Murder in the Philosophy of Nietzsche" in *Violence and Truth: On the Work of René Girard*, ed. Paul Dumouchel (London: Athlone Press, 1988), 1227–46.

8. Vattimo, *After Christianity*, 24.

9. R. Girard, *Things Hidden Since the Foundation of the World: Research Undertaken in Collaboration with J.-M. Oughourlian and G. Lefort*, trans. Stephen Bann and Michael Metteer (Stanford, Calif.: Stanford University Press, 1987). This English translation contains authorial revisions to the original French text: *Des choses cachées depuis la fondation du monde. Recherches avec Jean-Michel Oughourlian et Guy Lefort* (Paris: Grasset and Fasquelle, 1978).

10. Here and generally, translations of passages from the Bible are taken from *The Jerusalem Bible, Reader's Edition* (Garden City, N.Y.: Doubleday, 1971).

11. An interesting dialogue, starting from the theoretical premises of Girard, on the problem of the "two peaces," human and divine, is conducted by Mauro Ceruti and Giuseppe Fornari in *Le due paci. Cristianesimo e morte di Dio nel mondo globalizzato* (Milan: Cortina, 2005).

12. See "The Modern Concern for Victims," chapter 13 of Girard, *I See Satan Falling Like Lightning*, trans. James G. Williams (Maryknoll, N.Y.: Orbis Books, 2001), 161–69.

13. Santiago Zabala, "Introduction: A Religion Without Theists or Atheists" in *The Future of Religion*, by Richard Rorty and Gianni Vattimo, ed. Santiago Zabala (New York: Columbia University Press, 2005), 11–12.

14. Girard has recently discussed these matters in *Achever Clausewitz. Entretiens avec Benoît Chantre* (Paris: CarnetNord, 2008). An English translation is forthcoming from Michigan State University Press.

15. Girard, *I See Satan Falling*, 186. On this subject see W. Palaver, "Hobbes and the Katechon: The Secularization of Sacrificial Christianity," *Contagion* 2 (1995): 57–74.

16. Jacques Derrida and Gianni Vattimo, eds., *Religion*, trans. David Webb (Stanford, Calif.: Stanford University Press, 1998).

17. See Gianni Vattimo, *Belief*, trans. Luca D'Isanto and David Webb (Cambridge: Polity Press, 1999), 71–74.

18. See Rorty and Vattimo, *The Future of Religion*, 69.

19. Adopting Girard's theoretical premises, James Alison writes on sexual difference and the problem of homosexuality from a Christian and Catholic perspective in *Faith Beyond Resentment: Fragments Catholic and Gay* (London: Darton, Longman and Todd, 2001).

20. Vattimo, *After Christianity*, 99.

21. J. Habermas, "Notes on a Post-secular Society," Signandsight.com, June 18, 2008, http://www.signandsight.com/features/1714.html. The original German version, entitled "Die Dialektik der Säkularisierung," is also available online at http://www.blaetter.de/artikel.php?pr=2808. Full details about the lectures in which Habermas first presented these ideas, and links to

both the German and English versions, can be found on the Habermas Forum Web site, at http://www.habermasforum.dk/index.php?type=onlinetexts&text_id=422.

22. Ceruti and Fornari, *Le due paci*, 207.

23. On this, see René Girard with Pierpaolo Antonello and João Cezar de Castro Rocha, *Evolution and Conversion: Dialogues on the Origins of Culture* (London: Continuum, 2008), 238.

24. Vattimo, *After Christianity*, 101.

25. Vattimo, *After Christianity*, 95. This is a position that was also expressed by Jürgen Habermas and Joseph Ratzinger (now Pope Benedict XVI) in their 2004 dialogue, recently published in English; see Jürgen Habermas and Joseph Ratzinger, *The Dialectics of Secularization: On Reason and Religion* (Fort Collins, Colo.: Ignatius Press, 2007).

26. Giuseppe Fornari summarizes the matter thus in his discussion of sacrificial elements in pre-Christian culture: "The fact that we possess a cognitive tool unknown to the Greeks does not mean we have the right to think ourselves better than they and the same is true in regard to non-Christian cultures. Christianity's power of penetration has not been its particular cultural identity but its capacity to redeem the *whole* history of man, summing up and surpassing all its sacrificial forms. This is the real spiritual metalanguage that can describe and go beyond the language of violence" (G. Fornari, "Labyrinthine Strategies of Sacrifice: *The Cretans* by Euripides," *Contagion* 4 [1997]: 187).

1. CHRISTIANITY AND MODERNITY

1. René Girard with Pierpaolo Antonello and João Cezar de Castro Rocha, *Evolution and Conversion: Dialogues on the Origins of Culture* (London: Continuum, 2008), 257. Italics in the original.

2. Gianni Vattimo, *Belief*, trans. Luca D'Isanto and David Webb (Stanford, Calif.: Stanford University Press, 1999), 29. First publication: *Credere di credere* (Milan: Garzanti, 1996). The Italian title means "To believe that one believes."

3. Gianni Baget Bozzo (1925–2009) was an Italian priest and politician, of conservative orientation, who associated himself first with the Italian Socialist Party, in the late 1970s and 1980s, and later with Silvio Berlusconi's party, Forza Italia. In 1984 he was elected to the European Parliament in violation of the Catholic Church rule that forbids any cleric to hold political posts, and was suspended *a divinis* by Pope John Paul II. He published more than thirty books.

4. [When, in contexts such as this, Gianni Vattimo uses the verb *consumare* (to consume, use up, destroy), or the derived noun *consumazione* (the consumption, the finishing-off of something), or as in this case a phrase like "una dinamicità consumativa del Cristianesimo," they amount to technical terms within his philosophy and imply a reflexive shade of meaning. The title, and indeed the argument, of Stanley Fish's famous 1972 book of literary criticism, *Self-Consuming Artifacts*, come to mind. So I render the sense with phrases employing some variant of the adjective "self-consuming" or the noun "self-consumption."—WM]

5. Cesare Romiti was a major figure in Italian business. He was CEO of Alitalia (1969–1973) and FIAT (1996–1998) and was nicknamed Il Duro, or "The Tough Guy." The personal relationship between Cesare Romiti and Gianni Vattimo is not at all unfriendly, as readers will discover in Gianni Vattimo, with Piergiorgio Paterlini, *Not Being God*, trans. William McCuaig (New York: Columbia University Press, 2009).

6. Sergio Quinzio, *La sconfitta di Dio* (Milan: Adelphi, 1993). Sergio Quinzio (1927–1996) was an Italian theologian, author of more than twenty books. His most important work is *Commento alla Bibbia* (1972). His main tenet is that God's salvation is past hope because God is far from being omnipotent. The only hope for human kind is the coming of Christ's Kingdom.

7. The Lega Nord per l'indipendenza della Padania (Northern League for the Independence of the Po Valley region), a powerful force on the right wing of Italian politics, advocates local political autonomy, preservation of local tradition, and barriers to immigration.

8. Vincenzo Muccioli was an Italian philanthropist, founder of the "Comunità di San Patrignano," the biggest rehab community in Europe, with more than 2000 members. He was heavily criticized for his methods and was tried a few times for abuse. Allegedly, he used to chain some of the members of his community, and one occasion covered up the beating to death of one of them.

2. FAITH AND RELATIVISM

1. Dietrich Bonhoeffer, *Akt und Sein. Transzendentalphilosophie und Ontologie in der systematischen Theologie*, ed. Hans-Richard Reuter, *Werke*, vol 2 (1930; Munich: Kaiser Verlag, 1988), B.3.112: "Einen Gott, den 'es gibt,' gibt es nicht; Gott 'ist' im Perzonbezug, und das Sein ist sein Personsein." The corresponding English translation is Dietrich Bonhoeffer, *Act and Being: Transcendental Philosophy and Ontology in Systematic Theology*, ed. Wayne Whitson Floyd Jr., trans. H. Martin Rumscheidt, *Works*, vol. 2 (Minneapolis: Fortress Press, 1996), 115, and the passage reads in full: "There is no God who 'is there'; God 'is' in the relation

of persons, and being is God's being person." Vattimo renders the German phrase he quotes in Italian as: "Un Dio che 'c'è,' non c'è."

3. HERMENEUTICS, AUTHORITY, TRADITION

1. The moderator, Robert P. Harrison, is professor of Italian and French literature at Stanford University.

2. Ernst Bloch, *Geist der Utopie*, Faksimile der Ausgabe von 1918, *Gesamtausgabe*, vol. 16 (Frankfurt: Suhrkamp Verlag, 1971); see chap. 3, "Der Komische Held," 53–77, espeically 67–73, "Zur theorie des Dramas." This chapter does not appear in the second edition (1923) of *Geist der Utopie*, upon which translations into other languages are based. Hence it will not be found, for example, in Ernst Bloch, *The Spirit of Utopia*, trans. Anthony Nassar (Stanford, Calif.: Stanford University Press, 2000).

3. [The contrasting words in Italian are *superuomo* and *oltreuomo*, and this is not the first time in his writing and speaking that Vattimo has expressed a preference for the latter as a translation, or interpretation, of Nietzsche's *Übermensch*. The question becomes how to translate *oltreuomo* into English. In the past I have used "overman," which is certainly closer to the German word, but not necessarily to the Italian one, because *oltre* (from the Latin *ultra*) implies horizontal movement "beyond" or "past" a marker of some kind, not an ascent to a higher plane. What Vattimo interprets Nietzsche to mean is a type of mankind that has gone beyond or gone further than (*jenseits von*) what mankind has hitherto been. Hence the coinage "beyond-man."—WM]

4. Van A. Harvey is emeritus professor of theology at Stanford.

5. Martin Heidegger, *Beiträge zur Philosophie (Vom Ereignis)*, ed. F.-W. von Herrmann, *Gesamtausgabe*, vol. 65 (Frankfurt: Vittorio Klostermann, 1989); *Contributions to Philosophy: From Enowning*, trans. Parvis Emad and Kenneth Maly (Bloomington: Indiana University Press, 1989). And see the essay by Vattimo in this volume; and, further, Gianni Vattimo, *After Christianity*, trans. Luca D'Isanto (New York: Columbia University Press, 2002), 123–37.

6. Friedrich Gogarten, *Demythologizing and History*, trans. Neville Horton Smith (London: SCM Press, 1955). The original German title is *Entmythologisierung und Kirche* (1953), literally *Demythologizing and The Church*.

7. "Apophasis: denial of one's intention to speak of a subject that is at the same time named or insinuated" (*Random House Unabridged Dictionary*, 2nd ed.).

4. HEIDEGGER AND GIRARD:
KÉNOSIS AND THE END OF METAPHYSICS

1. René Girard, *Things Hidden Since the Foundation of the World: Research Undertaken in Collaboration with J.-M. Oughourlian and G. Lefort*, trans. Stephen Bann and Michael Metteer (Stanford, Calif.: Stanford University Press, 1987), 273 (from book 2, chap. 4).

2. See Martin Heidegger, *Einführung in die Metaphysik* (1935) , ed. P. Jaeger, *Gesamtausgabe*, vol. 40 (Frankfurt: Vittorio Klostermann, 1983); and Heidegger, "Logos" (1951), in *Vorträge und Aufsätze*, ed. F.-W. von Herrmann, *Gesamtausgabe*, vol. 7 (Frankfurt: Vittorio Klostermann, 2000), 211–34.

3. For an account of the meaning of *Verwindung*, see Gianni Vattimo, *The End of Modernity: Nihilism and Hermeneutics in*

Postmodern Culture, trans. Jon R. Snyder (Baltimore, Md.: Johns Hopkins University Press, 1991), 171–80.

4. Luigi Pareyson, *Estetica. Teoria della formatività* (1954; Milan: Bompiani, 1988), 75 ff.

5. "Das Sein eigens denken, verlangt, das Sein als den Grund des Seienden fahren zu lassen zugunsten des im Entbergen verborgen spielenden Gebens, d.h. des Es gibt" (Martin Heidegger, "Zeit und Sein" [1962], in *Zur Sache des Denkens*, ed. F.-W. von Herrmann, *Gesamtausgabe*, vol. 14 [Frankfurt: Vittorio Klostermann, 2007], 10). [The English translation-cum-paraphrase of the words quoted by Vattimo is partly his, partly mine. Compare Joan Stambaugh's translation of the whole sentence in Martin Heidegger, *On Time and Being*, trans. Joan Stambaugh (New York: Harper and Row, 1972), 6: "To think Being explicitly requires us to relinquish Being as the ground of beings in favor of the giving which prevails concealed in unconcealment, that is, in favor of the It gives."—WM]

6. Reiner Schürmann, *Heidegger on Being and Acting: From Principles to Anarchy*, trans. Christine-Marie Gros and Reiner Schürmann (Bloomington: Indiana University Press, 1987); first published as *Le principe d'anarchie. Heidegger et la question de l'agir* (Paris: Seuil, 1982).

5. NOT JUST INTERPRETATIONS, THERE ARE FACTS, TOO

1. Gianni Vattimo, *Beyond Interpretation: The Meaning of Hermeneutics for Philosophy*, trans. David Webb (Stanford, Calif.: Stanford University Press, 1997), 45 (Girard's italics).

2. Vattimo, *Beyond Interpretation*, "Preface," ix–x.

3. Vattimo, *Beyond Interpretation*, 50–51.

4. Gianni Vattimo, *Schleiermacher, filosofo dell'interpretazione* (Milan: Mursia, 1968).

5. Vattimo, *Beyond Interpretation*, 50.

6. See "The Non-sacrificial Death of Christ," in *Things Hidden Since the Foundation of the World: Research Undertaken in Collaboration with J.-M. Oughourlian and G. Lefort*, trans. Stephen Bann and Michael Metteer (Stanford, Calif.: Stanford University Press, 1987), 205–15 (in book 2, chap. 2).

7. R. Girard, "Mimetische Theorie und Theologie," in *Von Fluch und Segen der Sündenbocke. Raymund Schwager zum 60*, ed. J. Niewiadomski and W. Palaver (Vienna, Austria: Kulturverlag, 1995), 15–29.

8. *Je vois Satan tomber comme l'éclair* (Paris: Grasset 1999); published in English as *I See Satan Falling Like Lightning*, trans. James G. Williams (Maryknoll, N.Y.: Orbis Books, 2001).

9. Friedrich Nietzsche, *Writings from the Late Notebooks*, ed. Rüdiger Bittner, trans. Kate Sturge (Cambridge: Cambridge University Press, 2003), 139. For the original German, see Friedrich Nietzsche, *Nachgelassene Fragmente, Herbst 1885–Herbst 1887, Sämtliche Werke. Kritische Gesamtausgabe*, vol. 8.1, ed. Giorgio Colli, Mazzino Montanari, et al. (Berlin: De Gruyter, 1974), fragment 7[60], dating from the period between the end of 1886 and spring 1887. [In aphorism 22 in *Beyond Good and Evil*, which dates from the same period, Nietzsche says, in effect, that the view that there are no facts, only interpretations, may very well be no more than an interpretation itself—and if it is, "so much the better." Both passages are adduced by Vattimo in his oeuvre.—WM]

10. René Girard, *The Scapegoat*, trans. Yvonne Freccero (Baltimore, Md.: Johns Hopkins University Press, 1986), chaps. 5 and 6.

11. Sophocles, *Oedipe-Roi* (Paris: Le livre de poche, 1994), 137.

12. See Girard, *The Scapegoat*, chap. 2.

13. In the study of myth and the natural religions, the trickster is a divinity, a spirit, a human hero, or an anthropomorphic animal that plays tricks on a community by disobeying or violating its rules. In Greek mythology, the tricksters include Prometheus, Hephaestus, Ulysses, and Hermes, and in Celtic mythology, Puck. The Devil, of course, in all of his folkloric variants, plays the role of the trickster in popular Christian culture.

BIBLIOGRAPHY

Alison, James. *Faith Beyond Resentment: Fragments Catholic and Gay.* London: Darton, Longman and Todd, 2001.

Bloch, Ernst. *Geist der Utopie.* Faksimile der Ausgabe von 1918. *Gesamtausgabe,* vol. 16. Frankfurt: Suhrkamp Verlag, 1971.

——. *The Spirit of Utopia.* Trans. Anthony Nassar. Stanford, Calif.: Stanford University Press, 2000.

Bonhoeffer, Dietrich. *Act and Being: Transcendental Philosophy and Ontology in Systematic Theology.* Ed. Wayne Whitson Floyd Jr., trans. H. Martin Rumscheidt. *Works,* vol. 2. Minneapolis: Fortress Press, 1996.

——. *Akt und Sein. Transzendentalphilosophie und Ontologie in der systematischen Theologie.* 1930. Ed. Hans-Richard Reuter. *Werke,* vol. 2. Munich: Kaiser Verlag, 1980.

Ceruti, Mauro, and Giuseppe Fornari. *Le due paci. Cristianesimo e morte di Dio nel mondo globalizzato.* Milan: Cortina, 2005.

Derrida, Jacques, and Gianni Vattimo, eds. *Religion.* Trans. David Webb. Stanford, Calif.: Stanford University Press, 1998.

Fornari, Giuseppe. "Labyrinthine Strategies of Sacrifice: *The Cretans* by Euripides." *Contagion* 4 (1997): 163–88..

Gauchet, Marcel. *The Disenchantment of the World.* Foreword Charles Taylor, trans. Oscar Burge. Princeton, N.J.: Princeton University Press 1999.

Girard, René. *Achever Clausewitz. Entretiens avec Benoît Chantre*. Paris: CarnetNord, 2008.

——. *Des choses cachées depuis la fondation du monde. Recherches avec Jean-Michel Oughourlian et Guy Lefort*. Paris: Grasset and Fasquelle, 1978.

——. "The Founding Murder in the Philosophy of Nietzsche." In *Violence and Truth: On the Work of René Girard*, ed. Paul Dumouchel, 227-46. London: Athlone Press, 1988.

——. *I See Satan Falling Like Lightning*. Trans. James G. Williams. Maryknoll, N.Y.: Orbis Books, 2001.

——. *Je vois Satan tomber comme l'éclair*. Paris: Grasset 1999.

——. "Mimetische Theorie und Theologie." In *Von Fluch und Segen der Sündenbocke. Raymund Schwager zum 60*, ed. J. Niewiadomski and W. Palaver, 15-29. Vienna, Austria: Kulturverlag, 1995.

——. "Nietzsche and Contradiction." *Stanford Italian Review* 6, no. 1-2 (1986): 53-65.

——. *The Scapegoat*. Trans. Yvonne Freccero. Baltimore, Md.: Johns Hopkins University Press, 1986.

——. "Superman and the Underground: Strategies of Madness—Nietzsche, Wagner, and Dostoyevsky." *Modern Language Notes* 91 (1976): 1161-85.

——. *Things Hidden Since the Foundation of the World: Research Undertaken in Collaboration with J.-M. Oughourlian and G. Lefort*. Trans. Stephen Bann and Michael Metteer. Stanford, Calif.: Stanford University Press, 1987.

——. *Violence and the Sacred*. Trans. Patrick Gregory. Baltimore, Md.: Johns Hopkins University Press, 1977.

Girard, René, with Pierpaolo Antonello and João Cezar de Castro Rocha. *Evolution and Conversion: Dialogues on the Origins of Culture*. London: Continuum, 2008.

Gogarten, Friedrich. *Demythologizing and History*. Trans. Neville Horton Smith. London: SCM Press, 1955.

Habermas, Jürgen. "Notes on a Post-secular Society." Signandsight .com, June 18, 2008. http://www.signandsight.com/features/ 1714.html. German original: "Die Dialektik der Säkularisierung." http://www.blaetter.de/artikel.php?pr=2808.

Habermas, Jürgen, and Joseph Ratzinger. *The Dialectics of Secularization: On Reason and Religion*. Fort Collins, Colo.: Ignatius Press, 2007.

Heidegger, Martin. *Beiträge zur Philosophie (Vom Ereignis)*. Ed. F.-W. von Herrmann. *Gesamtausgabe*, vol. 65. Frankfurt: Vittorio Klostermann, 1989.

——. *Contributions to Philosophy: From Enowning*. Tran. Parvis Emad and Kenneth Maly. Bloomington: Indiana University Press, 1989.

——. *Einführung in die Metaphysik*. 1935. Ed. P. Jaeger. *Gesamtausgabe*, vol. 40. Frankfurt: Vittorio Klostermann, 1983.

——. "Logos." 1951. In *Vorträge und Aufsätze*, ed. F.-W. von Herrmann. *Gesamtausgabe*, vol. 7:211–34. Frankfurt: Vittorio Klostermann, 2000.

——. *On Time and Being*. Trans. Joan Stambaugh. New York: Harper and Row, 1972.

——. "Zeit und Sein." 1962. In *Zur Sache des Denkens*, ed. F.-W. von Herrmann. *Gesamtausgabe*, vol. 14. Frankfurt: Vittorio Klostermann, 2007.

Nietzsche, Friedrich. *Nachgelassene Fragmente, Herbst 1885–Herbst 1887. Sämtliche Werke. Kritische Gesamtausgabe*, vol. 8.1, ed. Giorgio Colli, Mazzino Montanari, et al. Berlin: De Gruyter, 1974.

——. *Writings from the Late Notebooks*. Ed. Rüdiger Bittner, trans. Kate Sturge. Cambridge: Cambridge University Press, 2003.

Palaver, W. "Hobbes and the Katechon: The Secularization of Sacrificial Christianity." *Contagion* 2 (1995): 57–74.

Pareyson, Luigi. *Estetica. Teoria della formatività*. 1954. Milan: Bompiani, 1988.

Quinzio, Sergio. *La sconfitta di Dio*. Milan: Adelphi, 1993.

Rorty, Richard, and Gianni Vattimo. *The Future of Religion*. Ed. Santiago Zabala. New York: Columbia University Press, 2005.

Schürmann, Reiner. *Heidegger on Being and Acting: From Principles to Anarchy*. Trans. Christine-Marie Gros and Reiner Schürmann. Bloomington: Indiana University Press, 1987.

——. *Le principe d'anarchie. Heidegger et la question de l'agir*. Paris: Seuil, 1982.

Sophocles. *Oedipe-Roi*. Paris: Le livre de poche, 1994.

Vattimo, Gianni. *After Christianity*. Trans. Luca D'Isanto. New York: Columbia University Press, 2002.

——. *Belief*. Trans. Luca D'Isanto and David Webb. Stanford, Calif.: Stanford University Press, 1999.

——. *Beyond Interpretation: The Meaning of Hermeneutics for Philosophy*. Trans. David Webb. Stanford, Calif.: Stanford University Press, 1997.

——. *Credere di credere*. Milan: Garzanti, 1996.

——. *The End of Modernity: Nihilism and Hermeneutics in Postmodern Culture*. Trans. Jon R. Snyder. Baltimore, Md.: Johns Hopkins University Press, 1991.

——. *Nihilism and Emancipation: Ethics, Politics, and Law*. Ed. Santiago Zabala. Trans. William McCuaig. New York: Columbia University Press, 2004.

——. *Schleiermacher, filosofo dell'interpretazione*. Milan: Mursia, 1968.

——. *The Transparent Society*. Trans. David Webb. Baltimore, Md.: Johns Hopkins University Press, 1994.

Zabala, Santiago. "Introduction: A Religion Without Theists or Atheists." In *The Future of Religion*, by Richard Rorty and Gianni Vattimo, ed. Santiago Zabala. New York: Columbia University Press, 2005.